Lecture Notes in Computer Science 6851

Commenced Publication in 1973
Founding and Former Series Editors:
Gerhard Goos, Juris Hartmanis, and Jan van Leeuwen

Eric W. Cooper   Victor V. Kryssanov
Hitoshi Ogawa   Stephen Brewster (Eds.)

Haptic and Audio Interaction Design

6th International Workshop, HAID 2011
Kusatsu, Japan, August 25-26, 2011
Proceedings

 Springer

Volume Editors

Eric W. Cooper
Victor V. Kryssanov
Hitoshi Ogawa
Ritsumeikan University
Faculty of Information Science and Engineering
1-1-1 Noji-Higashi
Kusatsu, Shiga, 525-8577, Japan
E-mail: {cooper, kvvictor, ogawa}@is.ritsumei.ac.jp

Stephen Brewster
University of Glasgow
School of Computing Science
Glasgow G12 8QQ, UK
E-mail: stephen.brewster@glasgow.ac.uk

ISSN 0302-9743   e-ISSN 1611-3349
ISBN 978-3-642-22949-7   ISBN 978-3-642-22950-3 (eBook)
DOI 10.1007/978-3-642-22950-3
Springer Heidelberg Dordrecht London New York

Library of Congress Control Number: 2011933342

CR Subject Classification (1998): H.5.2, H.1.2, H.5, I.3, K.4, I.5

LNCS Sublibrary: SL 3 –
Information Systems and Application, incl. Internet/Web and HCI

Typesetting: Camera-ready by author, data conversion by Scientific Publishing Services, Chennai, India

Printed on acid-free paper

Springer is part of Springer Science+Business Media (www.springer.com)

Preface

This volume comprises the papers presented at the 6th International Workshop on Haptic and Audio Interaction Design, HAID 2011, which took place during August 25–26 in Kusatsu, Japan.

Today's highly competitive yet saturated market of computer entertainment and mobile communication systems creates an ever-increasing demand for reconsidering the very foundations of user interfaces and information technologies. In striving to find ways to dramatically improve both the efficiency and the usability of computer systems, researchers in academia and industry have been quick to recognize the importance of multimodal interfaces and the crucial role that diverse modalities can play in user-system interactions. Since its inauguration in 2006, the International Workshop on Haptic and Audio Interaction Design (HAID) has been a notable international forum for discussing ideas, practical developments, and empirical observations related to novel aspects of the deployment of audio and haptic modalities in various user-system interaction scenarios. The succession of HAID annual conferences held in Glasgow, Seoul, Jyväskylä, Dresden, and Copenhagen delivered an impressive compilation of research results that have revealed numerous advantages and also highlighted problems associated with multi-modal interfaces. HAID 2011 continued the traditions of its five successful predecessors.

Each of the 22 full papers submitted to the workshop was carefully reviewed by at least three members of the International Program Committee. Given the interdisciplinary nature of the domain of human–machine interaction, additional reviewers had to be assigned in some cases, which resulted in several papers receiving evaluations by four or even five experts. Thirteen regular papers from institutions in six different countries were selected for presentation at HAID 2011 and, after revisions by the authors based on the reviewer comments, included in this volume. The workshop featured a keynote lecture by Hiroyuki Shinoda from the University of Tokyo on "Noncontact Haptic Interface Using Ultrasound." A summary of the lecture is also included in this publication.

The presented papers report on the most recent advances in theory, technology, and conceptual design of multimodal human–machine interactions. In the volume, the papers are divided into four categories. The first set of articles deals with haptic user interfaces. Karljohan Lundin Palmerius discusses the problem of modeling surfaces with varying stiffness and proposes an efficient algorithm for rendering virtual objects with such characteristics. Yugo Hayashi, Eric W. Cooper, Victor V. Kryssanov, and Hitoshi Ogawa investigate subjective interpretations of tactile perceptions of basic surfaces reproduced with PHAN-ToM Omni and develop a model for semantic characterization of the parameter space of this popular haptic display. Umut Koçak, Karljohan Lundin Palmerius, Camilla Forsell, Anders Ynnerman, and Matthew Cooper present their findings from an analysis of experiments conducted to explore various aspects of contact related to stiffness perception of virtual objects and their influences on the just noticeable difference (JND) of stiffness. Mikhail Svinin and Igor Goncharenko develop a model of human reaching movements for haptic manipulation of flexible objects and validate it via experiments. Yongjae Yoo, Inwook Hwang, and Seungmoon Choi exploit the analogy of chords in music and conduct experiments to investigate perceptual characteristics of various vibrotactile patterns and their consonance.

The next theme of audio interaction design is presented with two articles. Kota Nakano, Masanori Morise, and Takanobu Nishiura propose a real-time vocal manipulation system to improve subjective experiences of interactive karaoke and discuss the first user reactions to its implemented prototype. Antti Pirhonen and Kai Tuuri describe the novel concept of an interactive relaxation application, where interaction in the audio modality is aimed at regulating the user's breath rate, and discuss results of preliminary validation experiments.

The third category is composed of articles addressing cross- and multi-modal human–machine interactions. Sebastian Merchel, M. Ercan Altinsoy, and Maik Stamm present experimental findings related to cross-modal perception of vertical whole-body vibrations and tones from isophones. Andrea Bianchi, Ian Oakley, and Dong Soo Kwon propose an original authentication technique based on the use of simple audio or haptic cues and validate it via experiments. Marco Romagnoli, Federico Fontana, and Ratna Sarkar investigate vibrotactile recognition of musical scales produced by a harmonium in two different cultural settings and discuss their empirical results. Maik Stamm, M. Ercan Altinsoy, and Sebastian Merchel approach the problem of user orientation in a haptic virtual space and investigate whether providing acoustic localization cues in addition to haptic signals would assist the user.

While all the above studies deal with more or less well-established concepts and technologies of multimodal human–machine interaction, the last set of papers included in this volume presents new solutions that are not yet part of the domain's mainstream research. Tomasz M. Rutkowski describes the concept of the auditory brain–machine interface and also results of extensive experimentation with prototypes of its key elements. Hiroyuki Shinoda presents a novel technological solution for the creation of non-contact haptic interfaces and outlines major application areas for future deployment of such interfaces. Finally, Yusuke Kita and Yoshio Nakatani propose a system to manage and assist recollection of human memories that utilizes the olfactory modality, and discuss results of preliminary experiments with the system's prototype.

We believe that, as a whole, this compilation will be a useful source of information for researchers and developers of user interfaces and interaction systems, and we wish you interesting reading and a productive time ahead.

We would like to thank all the contributing authors, participants, and the organizers for making HAID 2011 possible in spite of the tragic consequences of the Great East Japan Earthquake that led to cancellations of many conferences in this country in 2011. Last but not least, we are grateful to the Program Committee members for their professional work in reviewing and defining the program of this workshop.

August 2011   Eric W. Cooper
                                                          Victor V. Kryssanov
                                                             Hitoshi Ogawa
                                                          Stephen Brewster

Organization

The 6th International Workshop on Haptic and Audio Interaction Design was organized by the following members, with support from Ritsumeikan University, Japan.

Conference Chairs

Victor V. Kryssanov   Ritsumeikan University, Japan
Stephen Brewster   University of Glasgow, UK

Program Chairs

Eric W. Cooper   Ritsumeikan University, Japan
Yoshio Nakatani   Ritsumeikan University, Japan

Posters and Demos Chair

Yugo Hayashi   Ritsumeikan University, Japan

Local Organizing Committee Chair

Hitoshi Ogawa   Ritsumeikan University, Japan

Local Organizing Committee

Kozaburo Hachimura   Ritsumeikan University, Japan
Yugo Hayashi   Ritsumeikan University, Japan
Hajime Murao   Kobe University, Japan
Frank Rinaldo   Ritsumeikan University, Japan
Tomasz M. Rutkowski   University of Tsukuba and RIKEN Brain
         Science Institute, Japan
Mikhail Svinin   Kyushu University, Japan
Ross Walker   Ritsumeikan University, Japan

Program Committee

Ercan Altinsoy   Dresden University of Technology, Germany
Stephen Barrass   University of Canberra, Australia
Stephen Brewster   University of Glasgow, UK
Seungmoon Choi   POSTECH, Korea

Cumhur Erkut	Aalto University, Finland
Frederico Fontana	University of Udine, Italy
Bruno Giordano	McGill University, Canada
Igor Goncharenko	I-Net Corp., Japan
Koh Kakusho	Kwansei Gakuin University, Japan
Yutaka Kanou	SoftCube Co., Japan
Charlotte Magnusson	Lund University, Sweden
David McGookin	University of Glasgow, UK
Rolf Nordahl	Aalborg University, Denmark
Ian Oakley	University of Madeira, Portugal
Antti Pirhonen	University of Jyväskylä, Finland
Roope Raisamo	University of Tampere, Finland
Tomasz M. Rutkowski	University of Tsukuba and RIKEN Brain Science Institute, Japan
Eva-Lotta Sallnas	Royal Institute of Technology, Sweden
Augusto Sarti	Politecnico di Milano, Italy
Stefania Serafin	Aalborg University, Denmark
Mikhail Svinin	Kyushu University, Japan
Hiromi Tanaka	Ritsumeikan University, Japan
Bill Verplank	Stanford University, USA
Patrice L. Tamar Weiss	University of Haifa, Israel

Sponsoring Institutions

Ritsumeikan University, Japan

Table of Contents

Emerging Multimodal Interaction Technologies and Systems

Adding Tangential Forces
in Lateral Exploration of Stiffness Maps

Karljohan Lundin Palmerius

C-Research
Linköping University, Sweden
karljohan.lundin.palmerius@liu.se

Abstract. We believe that the lateral exploration of surfaces with varying stiffness, *stiffness maps*, using computer generated haptics is an underestimated and important procedure with impact in many application
areas. Feeling the change of stiffness while sweeping the haptic probe over
a surface can potentially give an understanding of the spatial distribution
of this stiffness, however current algorithms lack tangential cues of stiffness changes. This introduces energy sources and sinks that potentially
affects the stability of the system, apart from being physically incorrect
and thus unrealistic. We discuss the forces and effects involved in the
exploration of stiffness maps and propose an energy-based algorithm for
tangential forces that augments the feedback from the map, in particular during lateral exploration. The algorithm is based on basic physical
principles and has the potential to increase both realism and stability.
A user study was conducted to analyze the effect of this algorithm on
stiffness perception.

Keywords: stiffness map, kinaesthetics, lateral forces, energy.

1   Introduction

The use of point-based, haptic interaction devices is a popular method of introducing touch in computer environment. These devices typically provide primarily
kinaesthetic feedback. The application area considered in this paper is the haptic rendering of surfaces with varying stiffness, *stiffness maps*, for example for
the purpose of medical palpation to identify sub surface structures or for data
exploration. The objective of palpation is typically to locate or assess the spatial
distribution of features. Our own interest in this is for the realistic rendering of
skin with the inclusion of bone and vessels for the probing for needle insertion.
Other interesting applications are the exploration of CT or MRI as presented
by Yano et al. in [15] and the exploration of nano surfaces captured through
scanning probe microscope as presented by Choi et al. in [5].

The exploratory procedures presented by Lederman and Klatzky in [10] indicate that the primary means of exploring stiffness is by applying *pressure* and
that *lateral motion* is used primarily to explore texture. Choi et al.[5], however,
provide an analysis of a topographic interpretation of stiffness maps during lateral motion that indicates an important connection between this exploratory

E.W. Cooper et al. (Eds.): HAID 2011, LNCS 6851, pp. 1–10, 2011.

procedure and the interpretation of stiffness. The different forces available in the exploration of stiffness maps and their implementation in computer generated feedback may have an impact on this interpretation. This paper provides an attempt at analyzing the forces involved.

We believe that lateral exploration of stiffness maps is an underestimated and important procedure with impact in many application areas. Feeling the change of stiffness while sweeping the haptic probe over a surface can potentially give an understanding of the spatial distribution of this stiffness. We propose an energy-based algorithm for tangential forces from stiffness maps that augments the feedback from stiffness maps, in particular during lateral exploration. The algorithm is based on physical principles and has the potential to increase both realism and stability by removing unnatural energy sources and sinks in the basic stiffness rendering.

The contributions of this paper are:

- an analysis of the haptic exploration of stiffness maps
- the proposal of an energy-based algorithm producing tangential forces from stiffness maps for increased realism and stability
- a study on the effect of such forces on the just noticeable stiffness difference (JND) during lateral exploration of stiffness maps

2   Background and Related Work

Though second to surgery simulation, the use of haptic techniques to simulate the procedure of palpation is quite common. Research in this area, however, largely overlaps with the research on surgery simulators, in that they are often based on soft body deformation models. There are also situations where the full dynamic simulation of soft tissues is not necessary for the conveying of plausible haptic sensation. In such situations off-the-shelf algorithms for surface rendering can be used for the general sensation of the palpated skin surface, overlayed with feedback specific to the current palpation simulation. An example of this is the palpation of femoral pulse by Coles et al.[6]. There the surface feedback is overlayed by force feedback simulating the pulse, as well as tactile feedback through piezoelectric elements on the finger tips.

The spring stiffness constant used in the typical surface rendering algorithm can be interpreted as reflecting the hardness of the rendered surface. By varying this constant over the simulated surface, a stiffness map, the sensation of varying hardness is achieved. Yano et al. use this technique to perceptualize the cross section of CT data or MRI[15]. The same year, Choi et al. presented a similar effort, however on scanning probe microscopy (SPM) data[5].

Choi et al. also showed that the topography of a surface may be misinterpreted if both the height of the surface and its stiffness varies spatially. In a continuing effort on this topic they compensate for this effect by adding a dynamic bias to the surface height so that the normal directed force is always the same during a purely lateral motion[2,4]. They have also experimented with using force shading to render the slant of the varying surface height[3].

3   Stiffness Exploration

Two approaches to exploring stiffness of surfaces are mainly considered in the literature. Applying pressure is described by the exploratory procedures presented by Lederman and Klatzky in [10] as the primary means of acquiring knowledge about object hardness. An alternative is the lateral exploration that may be important to assess the spatial distribution of any property, be it shape or temperature or, as in our case, stiffness. Here follows a discussion on the forces and effects involved in these procedures with a motivation for extending the typical rendering algorithm.

3.1   Surface Feedback

There are many variations of algorithms for producing haptic feedback from geometrical surfaces. The algorithms for point-based, kinaesthetic, impedance control haptic feedback, considered here can be considered to have evolved through three steps. First the *penalty method* was used[12,14]. In that approach the penetration of objects is penalized by a force feedback. The larger the penetration, the greater the force. The penalty method has been largely replaced by the *god-object method*[16,7] which removes the worst haptic artifacts associated with the penalty method. These appear primarily with thin objects and around sharp edges. Finally the *proxy-based approach*[13] was introduced by Ruspini et al. It works better with complex and dynamic polygonal objects and has therefore replaced the god-object method in some systems.

All these algorithms follow the same basic principle: the haptic probe penetrates the surface and a spring simulation, or equivalent in the form of for example a PI regulator, provides feedback that pushes the instrument towards the surface. The most elementary implementation of this is the penalty approach, which we will use as example in this paper. Here friction is ignored and the normal directed force feedback, $\mathbf{F}_N$, is calculated from the pure penetration of the surface,

$$\mathbf{F}_N = -k_s \left(\mathbf{x}_{\text{probe}} - \mathbf{x}_{\text{surface}} \right) \tag{1}$$

where k_s is the surface stiffness, $\mathbf{x}_{\text{probe}}$ is the position of the haptic probe and $\mathbf{x}_{\text{surface}}$ is the probe's projection onto the surface, representing the optimal virtual position of the haptic probe, see Fig. 1.

When this algorithm is used to render a stiffness map the surface stiffness property is defined as a function of the probe's projection on the surface,

$$\mathbf{F}_N = -k_s(\mathbf{x}_{\text{surface}}) \left(\mathbf{x}_{\text{probe}} - \mathbf{x}_{\text{surface}} \right) \tag{2}$$

This principle is similar in all algorithms mentioned above.

3.2   Pressure Procedure

During the pressure procedure the haptic probe is primarily moved in the direction of the normal of the surface. The real world equivalent would be the

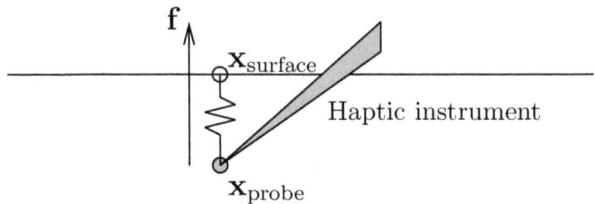

Fig. 1. The principle of the penalty method: the penetration of the surface is penalized with an increasing opposing force according to Hooke's law

compression of a deformable object. The stiffness of the object is perceived as a force/displacement relationship during this exploration, primarily the change in force caused by change in compression. An alternative model is presented by Lawrence et al. in [9]. Their *rate-hardness* model identifies surface hardness as the initial rate of force change (N/s) relative the penetration velocity (m/s).

Regardless of model, the main cue is normal directed force change due to normal direction motion. In interaction and exploration with distribution stiffness, as with the topical stiffness map, the user is forced to focus on normal directed motion. Thus, the exploration of stiffness *distribution* will be performed by sampling at discrete points through pressure. This requires the user to explicitly remember multiple discrete data points and mentally merge these into a continuous visualization of the stiffness distribution.

3.3   Lateral Exploration

An alternative exploration of a stiffness map would be using lateral motion. With this approach the user can perceive the change of stiffness over the spatial region of the chosen path of exploration. The change of procedure, however, is bound to change the perception of the surface stiffness, as indicated by Lederman and Klatzky's exploratory procedures ([10]).

Normal Directed Forces. There will be normal directed forces regardless of the exploratory procedure used. When the primary motion is lateral over the surface, however, the change in penetration depth is small compared to the general motion. Thus the highly dynamic and low resolution sense of proprioception may have problems associating the normal directed change of force with this change in penetration depth. The research of Choi et al.[5] indicates that the perception of stiffness as a force/displacement relationship diminishes during lateral exploration and that other cues become more important. They showed that the probing hand is subconsciously moved in a way so that the applied normal force is held constant during lateral exploration. In such situations the primary perception is the change of penetration depth, which was shown to be interpreted as changes in the topography of the surface. We have conducted an informal experiment that confirm this sensation and it is at the same time consistent with

Lederman and Klatzky's exploratory procedure called *contour following*. There is no reason to suspect that a user would be incapable of interpreting such sense of changes in surface height as changes in stiffness, however in the interaction of both changing topography and stiffness there is little chance of telling these cues apart.

In their work Choi et al. change the height of the surface in the haptic algorithm to compensate for the perceived change in height caused by the change in stiffness. This allowed for a better interpretation of the topography, however will at the same time remove a cue of stiffness change. An informal experiment confirms that a user has to resort to the pressure procedure to be able to feel changes in the stiffness map when height compensation is activated. This is of course a trade-off strongly dependent on the application at hand.

Tangential Forces. Current implementations of stiffness maps do not provide any tangential forces as response to changes in the stiffness over the surface, however such forces do exist in reality. On a frictionless surface a finger pushing into the surface will be moved by tangential forces into a local stiffness minimum. This is shown through physical equations in the following section and to allow for effective exploration of stiffness with also lateral motion the system should provide these tangential cues of stiffness variation.

4   Energy-Based Tangential Force

Without tangential forces the exploration of a surface with varying stiffness will introduce energy sources and sinks without physical counterparts. The algorithm for a tangential feedback force presented in this paper is based on removing this energy, leading to conservation of energy in the system.

Compressing a surface and then moving the probe laterally from one area into another with higher stiffness will store potential energy. The spring-based potential energy, $E_p(\mathbf{x})$, for the feedback at a point on the surface, $\mathbf{x}$, is expressed as

$$E_p(\mathbf{x}) = \int_0^D k_{\mathrm{s}}(\mathbf{x})r \, \mathrm{d}r = k_{\mathrm{s}}(\mathbf{x})D^2/2 \qquad (3)$$

where k_{s} is the stiffness map, a function in $\mathbb{R}^2$ over the surface, and D is the current penetration depth, $D = |\mathbf{x}_{\mathrm{probe}} - \mathbf{x}_{\mathrm{surface}}|$. Changing stiffness over lateral motion results in change of potential energy. If this motion is allowed without tangential force, the added energy will not correspond to dissipated energy anywhere else violating the conservation of energy in the system. The energy flow is equal to the force integrated along the path so it follows, by spatial derivation, that

$$\nabla E(\mathbf{x}) = \mathbf{F}(\mathbf{x}) \qquad (4)$$

where $\mathbf{F}$ is the force corresponding to the change in energy. Combining Eqn. 4 and 3, while changing the sign to make it *remove* energy, we get

$$\mathbf{F}_{\mathrm{T}}(\mathbf{x}) = -\nabla k_{\mathrm{s}}(\mathbf{x})D^2/2 \qquad (5)$$

where $\mathbf{F}_T$ is the tangential force required to compensate for the energy flow due to the surface compression during lateral exploration. The del operator is operating in 2D, since k_s is a function defined in 2D, and $\mathbf{F}_T$ will therefore always be tangential to the surface.

Calculating the final force feedback is straightforward. We estimate the gradient of the stiffness map using Gaussian weighted central difference. Then, for the penalty-based approach used here, the energy conserving tangential force, $\mathbf{F}_T$, is simply combined by vector addition with the normal directed force. For god-object or proxy-based approaches, the calculated force is instead used to modulate the proxy motion over the surface, together with other modulating effects such as friction or bump maps. This approach should be fully compatible with varying geometrical structures as well as force shading[13].

This algorithm has several qualities: it is based on simple physical facts and therefore more realistic by definition, it is very straightforward in its mathematical and algorithmic appearance and thus also easy to implement. With this algorithm in place moving the haptic probe laterally with constant penetration depth from a soft area into a stiffer area, for example, gives a resistance providing the sense of loading a spring. This energy is then released and absorbed by the user when moving the haptic probe to a level with the original stiffness.

5   User Study

The added tangential force makes, by physical definition, the feedback more realistic. In the context of lateral exploration for the purpose of surface examination, however, we wish to analyze how the perception of the stiffness variation is affected. This study aims at testing if the just-noticeable-difference quality (JND) is affected by the tangential force with everything else left identical. A result where the increased realism comes with no or little deterioration of perception would be considered a good result, an improvement would be optimal and a significant deterioration would be a strong contraindication for the use of this algorithm for most applications.

5.1   Software and Settings

The presented algorithm was implemented in a very simplistic computer program allowing only a flat surface, no friction and an image-based stiffness map. The system was implemented in H3D API but without using their surface rendering capabilities. The system runs on a haptic workstation equipped with a Desktop PHANToM device from Sensable and a stereoscopic CRT monitor showing visual rendering for navigation. The graphics provide no cues of stiffness during the experiment.

Method. The study follows a within-subject design with one independent variable having two levels: normal directed force only (N) and normal directed and tangential forces (N+T). We apply the psycho-physical staircase procedure[11], which is designed to gradually advance towards a stimuli level at which the subject can, to a certain degree, identify the strongest stimuli among a certain amount of choices. This study apply four alternatives forced choice (4-AFC) with a one up two down staircase, with termination after six reversals and using the mean of the last three reversals as result level.

We apply an adaptive approach[8] to control the step size in the staircase. This improves the convergence while maintaining high precision in the final result. The experiment uses an initial step size of 5 percentage points and ends up with a step size of 1 percentage point before the last reversals.

Procedure. The subjects were confronted with a square surface with five regions, see Fig. 2. Four grey corner squares represent the choices. Three of these regions have the base stimuli level and one is harder than the other. A base level of 200 N/m was chosen since this provides considerable feedback at moderate surface penetration while being well within the stability range for the haptic device even for a high stimuli level. The white centre cross is 20% softer than the base level and functions as an intermediate blank to remove direct comparison between the patches.

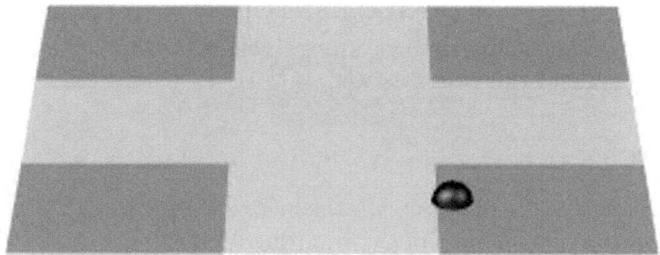

Fig. 2. This image shows the important part of the screen during the experiment. Three of the four grey squares are of base stiffness and a randomly selected one is stiffer. The white cross is softer and removes direction comparison between patches. The small sphere is the graphical representation of the haptic probe.

The subjects explored the surface laterally with no explicit normal motion which was controlled by a supervisor. They were not introduced to the difference between the conditions, knowledge that one is more physically correct could add a bias, and the order of appearance was balanced. The objective was to find the harder patch. Its correct location was randomized and the selection was done by pressing a button on the haptic instrument on the chosen patch.

As an initial search for an entry level the task was first very simple, the harder surface being 100% stiffer than base stiffness. This was then quick lowered by halving the difference for every second right answer until two consecutive wrong answers were given. The mean of the last successful and the failed difference was calculated and the staircase was initialized at this level, following with the adaptive approach from there. This approach proved very effective with very few subjects deviating more than one or two initial step sizes from their starting points. The test took approximately 20 minutes.

Participants. Ten subjects, aged 25–34, took part in the evaluation. They have all technical background but varying experience of computer simulated haptics. No monetary compensation was issued.

5.2   Pre-test Analysis and Hypothesis

Preliminary tests showed very little difference between the conditions. Possibly the N condition could perform somewhat better than the N+T condition. This suggests that primarily the sense of height difference is used to determine the stiffness and that the tangential forces may obscure this sensation. A hypothesis that the N condition performs better than the N+T condition is suggested, which would then support this theory. Since the preliminary tests are inconclusive to whether this is a good hypothesis we also suggest the contradictory hypothesis, that the N+T condition performs better than the N condition.

We prepared to test these hypotheses for statistical significance using the dependent t-test. This test takes into account the individual differences and is therefore useful when the performance varies a lot between subjects. Also, because of important shortcomings in significance tests[1], we choose to show prediction intervals of the result as well.

5.3   Results

The mean of the four last reversals was taken for each subject. A simple statistical analysis of the basic properties of the resulting JND data over all subjects yields a mean of 16.3% and 8.4% for the N and N+T conditions, respectively, and a standard deviation of 22.1% and 4.2%, respectively. Before further statistical analysis can be conducted the logarithm is applied to the data to remove the skew inherent to the nature of the data and transform it into a Normal distribution. The 95% confidence intervals of the mean JND for the individual conditions are 5.1%–19.5% for the N condition and 5.1%–10.8% for the N+T condition.

A dependent t-test shows that the difference of mean JND between the two conditions is not statistically significant with $p = 0.22$. This is with a two-tailed test since both hypotheses are tested simultaneously. The two one-tailed tests, however, are not significant either. Thus, both stated hypotheses are rejected: the difference between the conditions is too likely to be the result of noise to be considered statistically assured.

A confidence interval over the relationship will, since we applied the logarithm, be expressed as the quotient of the JND means, $\frac{N+T}{N}$. With 95% confidence the quotient between the means lies within the range 0.45–1.23. This shows why there is no statistical significance of the difference between the conditions, since 1.0 is included in the range. Interesting, however, is that the upper limit is not very high. With a one-sided confidence limit we find out that with 95% confidence the JND for condition N+T is not more than 11.8% worse than that of N.

6 Discussion and Conclusions

The mean JND for lateral exploration with both normal directed and tangential forces, using the energy-based algorithm, was shown to be at most 11.8% worse than that of exploration with normal directed forces alone, with a confidence level of 95%. Observe that this is percentage of JND, *not* percentage points. This is a side effect of using the logarithm for transforming the data with the logarithm. As an illustrative but purely hypothetical example, if the mean JND for the N condition happens to be 16.3%, then the JND for the N+T condition is *at most* 20.0%, a mere 3.7 percentage points difference at that level, with 95% confidence.

These results indicate that the increased realism provided by the presented algorithm comes with no or little deterioration of the JND between stiffness levels during lateral exploration of a surface. While the optimal outcome was not shown in this study, that the algorithm provides improved perception of JND, this is still a positive result showing that this algorithm can be used to increase the realism and stability without fear of a large deterioration of the feedback quality. The lack of improvement can possibly be explained by the interpretation of stiffness change as topographic change. Haptic shape cues are strong and since we used no height compensation[2] their effect may overshadow any improvement caused by the lateral forces.

We have presented a physics-based, elementary and easy to implement algorithm introducing tangential feedback during the exploration of stiffness maps, and discussed how this is of special importance during lateral exploration. This algorithm is shown to remove energy sources and sinks in stiffness maps which is anticipated to improve both realism and stability. We have also studied whether the increased realism comes with a penalty or improvement on the JND during lateral exploration. The results indicate that the effect, if any, is small and that the conclusive characterization of it would require a larger study. This study, however, shows that the algorithm at most worsen the perception with 11.8% with a confidence level of 95%, possibly even improving it.

Adding this tangential cue for stiffness change over lateral exploration may also remove the importance of the height cues described in section 3.3. Testing simultaneous topographic and stiffness exploration with height compensation and energy-based tangential forces is an interesting future project on this topic.

Acknowledgements. This work has been supported by the Swedish Research Council in the Linnaeus Centre CADICS, and by Swedish Foundation for Strategic Research in the centre MOVIII.

References

1. Armstrong, J.S.: Significance tests harm progress in forecasting. International Journal of Forecasting 23, 321–327 (2007)
2. Cheon, J., Choi, S.: Perceptualizing a "Haptic edge" with varying stiffness based on force constancy. In: Pan, Z., Cheok, D.A.D., Haller, M., Lau, R., Saito, H., Liang, R. (eds.) ICAT 2006. LNCS, vol. 4282, pp. 392–405. Springer, Heidelberg (2006)

3. Cheon, J., Choi, S.: Haptizing a surface height change with varying stiffness based on force consistency: Effect of surface normal rendering. In: Proceedings of the World Haptics Conference (2007)
4. Cheon, J., Hwang, I., Han, G., Choi, S.: Haptizing surface topography with varying stiffness based on force constancy: Extended algorithm. In: Proceedings of the Symposium on Haptic Interfaces for Virtual Environment and Teleoperator Systems (2008)
5. Choi, S., Walker, L., Tan, H.Z., Crittenden, S., Reifenberger, R.: Force constancy and its effect on haptic perception of virtual surfaces. ACM Transactions on Applied Perception 2(2), 89–105 (2005)
6. Coles, T., John, N.W., Gould, D.A., Caldwell, D.G.: Haptic palpation for the femoral pulse in virtual interventional radiology. In: Proceedings of Advances in Computer-Human Interactions (2009)
7. Hutchins, M.: A constraint equation algebra as a basis for haptic rendering. In: Proceedings of Phantom User Group Workshop (2000)
8. Klymenko, V., Pizer, S.M., Johnston, R.E.: Visual psychophysics and medical imaging: Nonparametric adaptive method for rapid threshold estimation in sensitivity experiments. IEEE Transactions on Medical Imaging 9(4), 353–365 (1990)
9. Lawrence, D.A., Pao, L.Y., Dougherty, A.M., Salada, M.A., Pavlou, Y.: Rate-hardness: A new performance metric for haptic interfaces. IEEE Transactions on Robotics and Automation 16(4), 357–371 (2000)
10. Lederman, S.J., Klatzky, R.L.: Hand movements: A window into haptic object recognition. Cognitive Psychology 19(3), 342–368 (1987)
11. Levitt, H.: Transformed up-down methods in psychoacoustics. The Journal of the Acoustical Society of America 49(2), 467–477 (1971)
12. Massie, T.H., Salisbury, J.K.: The phantom haptic interface: A device for probing virtual objects. In: Proceedings of the ASME Winter Annual Meeting, Symposium on Haptic Interfaces for Virtual Environment and Teleoperator Systems (1994)
13. Ruspini, D.C., Kolarov, K., Khatib, O.: The haptic display of complex graphical environments. Computer Graphics 31(Annual Conference Series), 345–352 (1997)
14. Salisbury, K., Brock, D., Massie, T., Swarup, N., Zilles, C.: Haptic rendering: Programming touch interaction with virtual objects. In: Proceedings of the 1995 Symposium on Interactive 3D Graphics (1995)
15. Yano, H., Nudejima, M., Iwata, H.: Development of haptic rendering methods of rigidity distribution for tool-handling type haptic interface. In: Proceedings of the World Haptics Conference (2005)
16. Zilles, C.B., Salisbury, J.K.: A constraint-based god-object method for haptic display. In: Proceedings of IEE/RSJ International Conference on Intelligent Robots and Systems, Human Robot Interaction, and Cooperative Robots, vol. 3, pp. 146–151 (1995)

Semantic Parameterization of Basic Surface Models Rendered with PHANToM Omni

Yugo Hayashi, Eric W. Cooper, Victor V. Kryssanov, and Hitoshi Ogawa

College of Information Science and Engineering
Ritsumeikan University
Kusatsu, Shiga, 525-8577 Japan
yhayashi@fc.ritsumei.ac.jp,
{cooper,kvvictor,ogawa}@is.ritsumei.ac.jp

Abstract. This paper presents a study of subjective responses to haptic stimuli displayed as surfaces on a haptic force feedback device and a computer monitor and experienced through free kinesthetic exploration. The modified settings were stiffness, static friction, and dynamic friction as defined in the PHANToM Omni standard SDK. A sphere was used as the virtual shape for exploration. Subjects spoke freely about their subjective responses while session moderators recorded the comments as text. The responses were broken down and categorized by morphological analysis of haptic sensation primitives: hardness, softness, roughness, smoothness, and elasticity. Analysis of the resulting morphemes showed that eliciting specific subjective outcomes in kinesthetically experienced haptic space requires adjustment of multiple settings. Naïve understandings of haptic materials surface settings in such devices are likely to be insufficient. Open ended semantic studies such as the one described in this paper can result in a better understanding of this perceptual space and lead to better guidelines or supportive systems for haptic interface developers.

Keywords: subjective haptics, haptic materials settings, friction, stiffness.

1   Background and Motivation

Designers of interfaces that employ haptic modalities require models of user subjective response for many purposes, including real-world fidelity, affective product design, and descriptive instruction. In the past decades, there have been many studies in physical surface texture sensations but the work was not followed up by studies on the haptic displays now commonly available, nor has there been a systematic study of the subjective responses to specific surface characteristic settings on these devices. Models of subjective response are necessary not only for systems designed to achieve specific subjective results but, more importantly, for the designers of various haptic interfaces who would then have a common reference layer of subjective interpretations for virtual surface characteristics.

There has been a considerable amount of research elucidating the physical and neurological basis of tactile and haptic sensations. Lederman and Klatsky gave a gentle introduction, including multimodal aspects of haptic interactions [1]. They also

E.W. Cooper et al. (Eds.): HAID 2011, LNCS 6851, pp. 11–21, 2011.

briefly outlined some work in affective responses, specifically emotions. However, such work does not provide interface designers with insight about the subjective response a user is likely to have for any specific device setting. After understanding the basic psychophysical processes of kinesthetically interactive haptics, and before moving on to higher cognitive aspects, such as affective response, designers of both experimental and applied interactions need a method for defining the qualitative dimensions of haptic sensation, their orientation, and, eventually, useful quantitative models relative to common software used to define interactions. In other words, when designers choose parameters for surface characteristics, they need a method to describe how it would feel to the users.

Another area that has received significant attention in research has been to match sensations experienced with haptic devices to those experienced with real-world objects. One complaint about this research from those needing to build applications has been that proposed models have been constructed from data or knowledge collected from expert users rather than from the psychophysical models, from real-life objects, or from groups of "ordinary" non-expert users [2]. The psychophysical background has extended into studies of subjective responses to interaction with actual objects. Especially, researchers have sought to model the perceptual dimensions and scaling relating to the sensations of roughness and hardness. Works [3], [4], and [5] describe studies on physical objects to model subjective response. There are, however, many objectives still not met in these models, including the clarification of other subjective aspects of perceptual spaces in sensations experienced with interfaces built around haptic force feedback displays. There is, therefore, a need for the development of new models that would be applicable to both virtual environments, intended to mimic real-world experiences, and more abstract applications of haptic sensation in design, as discussed in [6] and [7].

Because of the developmental and cognitive relationships between tactile sensations and emotive or affective responses, there have been studies of subjective responses in dimensions of emotional category models. Although a few have touched on the issue of quantifying the subjective haptic responses at various settings [8], [9], the proposed theories do not generally attempt to characterize the ordinary non-emotional sensations experienced as physical touch. In order to satisfactorily quantify subjective responses, first it must be established whether users, from a relatively homogeneous social group, respond similarly to similar stimuli rendered with a typical haptic force feedback interface. There are also two open questions about the range of user responses. Model developers and system designers need to know the overall range of subjective responses as a proxy for understanding the general range of subjective sensations the device could be used to communicate.

The goal of the presented work is to lay a foundation for a quantitative model of semantic responses to haptic sensations experienced for a three-dimensional surface form expressed in interactions with a popular force feedback display and graphic user interface, specifically the semantic characterization of the PHANToM Omni parameter space, as defined with the standard SDK [10]. The model is to connect settings related to modeling surface stiffness and friction to possible subjective responses.

This paper thus describes experiments in which subjects experience the kinesthetic haptic sensation of touching a 3D object displayed in a graphic interface and rendered on a PHANToM Omni force feedback device. Each time, the surface characteristics for stiffness, static friction, and dynamic friction are randomized and recorded. The subject speaks freely about the sensation and these semantic phrases are recorded as text. The resulting text data is morphologically analyzed and keywords are extracted to form a basic model of semantic responses to the interactive experience. Section 2 describes the experiments. Section 3 gives the experimental results. Section 4 proposes a model of subjective semantic response of young Japanese subjects to the given kinesthetic haptic interaction with the PHANToM Omni display. This section also discusses the conclusions drawn from the study's results and outlines directions for future work.

2 Methods

The experiments described in this paper collected subjects' open-ended, subjective responses to a typical interaction with a PHANToM Omni haptic device. The interaction is touching a virtual sphere displayed both on an ordinary computer monitor and in a 3D haptic space by the Omni device. The standard SDK (OpenHaptics Toolkit [10]) was used to create the software used in the experiment. For each experimental session, settings were randomized for surface parameters of stiffness, dynamic friction, and static friction. Subjects were instructed to comment on their impressions during the interactive sessions and their comments were recorded as text.

These experiments were intended to explore as much of the perceptual space as practically possible in one study while still gaining applicable data. Each of the randomized settings was normalized and split into three ranges: low, medium, and high, as shown in Table 1. All of the permutations of these sets were tested and each specific setting within a given range was randomized to produce the parameters used in one session. The three ranges for each of the three modified parameters gave a total of 27 basic experimental setting types and every subject completed all the 27 range combinations.

Table 1. Settings were randomized within the given ranges, all bounding values inclusive

Setting range	Minimum	Maximum	Label
Low	0.03	0.15	L
Medium	0.3	0.6	M
High	0.85	1.0	H

Preliminary experiments with various shapes showed that subjects experienced different shapes differently, even for the same settings. Responses of hardness were stronger in shapes with edges or discontinuities (e.g. as in the case of modeling a plane spanning all virtual space rendered). With the objective of this study being to examine the settings for surfaces rather than edges, a sphere was used for the shape. The subject was instructed to observe a sphere displayed on a computer monitor. The sphere's gray, non-reflective surface was illuminated with ambient light, as shown in Fig. 1. The subject was then instructed to hold the haptic device and touch the sphere's surface by moving the PHANToM's stylus and viewing the haptic interface pointer (HIP) as it "touched" the surface on the visual display. The subjects were free to move the stylus in any way they felt would be the best to experience the surface quality of the virtual object.

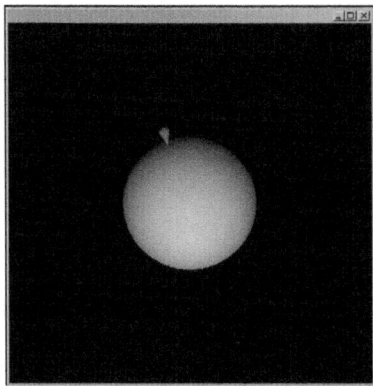

Fig. 1. The graphic interface of the experimental setup

For each specific stimulus setting, after viewing the 3D shape on the monitor and experiencing the shape using the stylus, the subjects were instructed to report any physical sensations or impressions for the given setting. A second participant, the moderator, coordinated the experiment procedure and recorded the subject's spoken verbal responses as text. Neither the subject nor the moderator knew any details of the virtual surface models used. The subjects and moderators were discouraged from recording metaphors, such as similes, and only to record descriptive terms. The moderator recorded all relevant monologues, in text form on a separate computer. All of the experiments were completed in Japanese. 35 undergraduate and graduate students (25 male and 10 female, average age 21.3 years old) participated in the experiments for a total of 945 recorded sessions and more than 5,000 semantic phrases, of which about 3,300 were extracted as adjective or noun phrases in the subsequent morphological analysis, described in the following section. All the subjects and moderators were native Japanese speakers with no prior experience of haptic interface and were not compensated for their participation. As no specific time limits were set, it took from 24 to 47 minutes (average time = 31 min.) per subject to complete all 27 sessions.

3 Results and Analysis

The recorded texts were broken down into morphemes with the Japanese morphological analysis tool MeCab (Java Sen port) [11], [12]. This linguistic analysis software is commonly used for extracting Japanese keywords indicating specific affective response in interactions [13]. The objective of the first stage of the analysis was to simply extract the keywords indicating semantic response labels.

MeCab software is capable of performing complete morphological analysis of Japanese natural language [12]. In the presented study, this tool was used to extract and label the verbal responses to the experiment described in the previous section. MeCab was first used to give a frequency count of all expressions recorded, over 5000 terms. Of these, MeCab then categorized about 3,000 responses as adjective, verb, noun, and adverb terms, 246 different terms total.

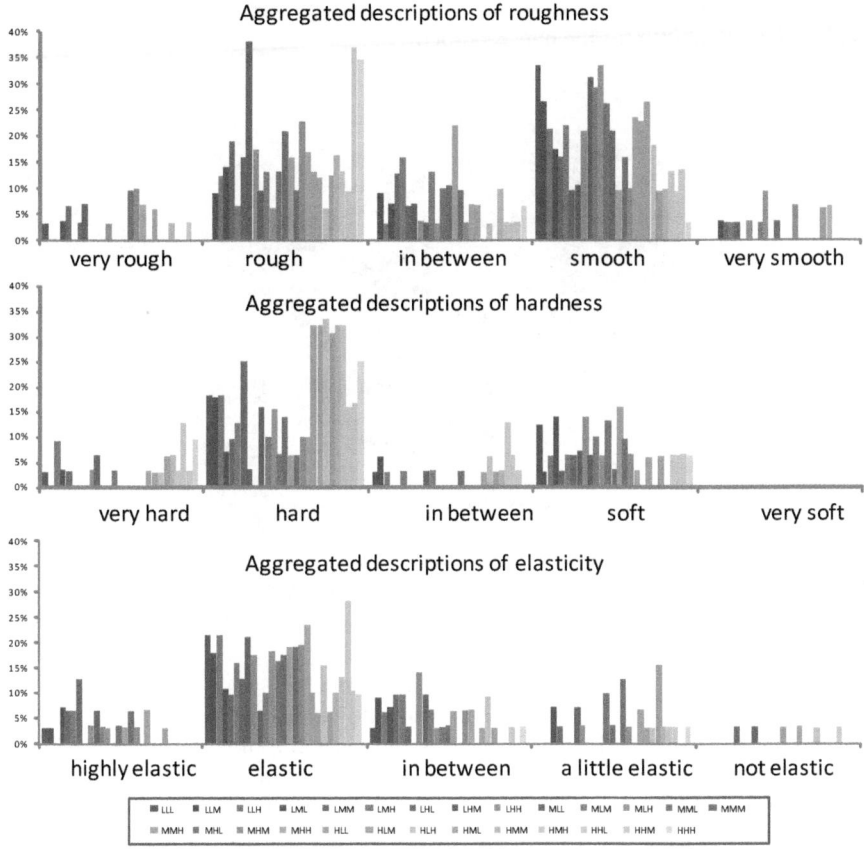

Fig. 2. Classification of reported perceptions by morphological analysis shows that all sets evoked strong response and that the responses were spread throughout the selected classes. The labels (LLL, LLM, etc.) give the settings for the stiffness, static friction, and dynamic friction parameters, respectively, as specified in Table 1. Values shown are percentage points of all categorized responses recorded for a given setting combination.

The next step was to label each of the terms as a haptic response keyword or as an adverb related to a haptic response term. The majority of the terms were haptic response keywords and were readily identified as belonging to three basic surface sensation types: hard to soft, smooth to rough, and high elasticity to low elasticity. A few terms were not classified on these axes, most notably those that were related to (or might be categorized as belonging to) a heavy to light axis. (All terms are given here as English translations for reference only, as such brief translations between different languages may not necessarily be accurate.) The adverb terms were nearly all readily classified along a single axis, indicating strength or intensity of the haptic response. These terms were used to weight the haptic responses positively or negatively and included phrases corresponding approximately to English terms such as very, a lot, a little, slightly, not so, etc. The procedures described in this section categorized, classified, and labeled 851 of the original 945 experiment sessions completed by the 35 subjects, successfully including more than 90% of the data recorded.

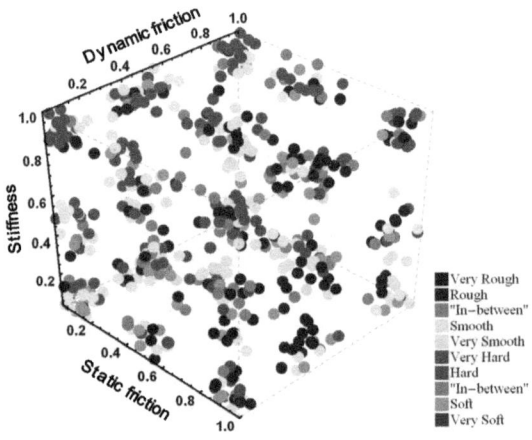

Fig. 3. Subjective semantic responses plotted in the PHANToM Omni standard parameter space show clusters for roughness and hardness, whereas perceptions of smoothness and softness appeared more evenly distributed

Histograms of the categorized responses are shown in Fig. 2 in an aggregated form. Each vertical axis shows the ratio of terms in every combination used (LLL, LLM, etc). Each horizontal axis shows the coded terms with the labels indicating the combinations of the objective parameters used to render the stimuli. The expected responses were those hypothesized to be related to the stiffness setting and the two friction settings, namely responses of hard-soft and rough-smooth. There were also frequently reported terms related to elasticity, which was not one of the expected responses as no elasticity related parameters were explicitly used to render the surfaces. A Spearman's rank correlation analysis showed that the values of the stiffness coefficient and the values of the static friction coefficient were both weakly correlated with subjective response (r=0.071 and r=-0.11, respectively; n=851; p<.01). No correlation was detected between the dynamic friction coefficient values and the subjective responses obtained.

Shown in Fig. 3 are all but the elasticity-related responses plotted on the three dimensions of haptic materials settings. Several fuzzy clusters can be observed for each of the expected response categories ('hard', 'soft', 'rough', and 'smooth') that nevertheless have no clear boundaries.

Three ANOVA (analysis of variance) were performed between the haptic materials settings (stiffness, static friction, and dynamic friction coefficient values) and the three pairs of haptic sensations most reported: (1) 'rough' and 'smooth', (2) 'hard' and 'soft', and (3) 'elastic' and 'inelastic'. On conducting the analysis, the reported sensations in each of the three groups were divided into two larger categories. The haptic sensations in (1) were categorized in the following way: 'very rough' and 'rough' as 'rough', and 'smooth' and 'very smooth' as 'smooth,' thus excluding the largely indeterminate responses of the in-between category. The haptic sensations in (2) and (3) were similarly categorized: 'very hard' and 'hard' as 'hard', 'soft' and 'very soft' as 'soft', 'highly elastic' and 'elastic' as 'elastic', and 'not very elastic' and 'not elastic' as 'inelastic'.

In the first 2×2 ANOVA, the first factor was the haptic sensation pair 'rough' and 'smooth'. The second factor was the haptic virtual materials settings (stiffness, static friction, and dynamic friction coefficients). The interaction between the two factors was found to be significant ($F(1,638)=7.5$, $p<.01$). Next, to investigate the differences of haptic sensations on each materials setting, an analysis of the simple main effect was conducted. Results indicate that the stiffness setting was higher when 'rough' was reported than when 'smooth' was ($F(1,957)=5.25$, $p<.05$). The static friction setting was also higher for 'rough' than for 'smooth' ($F(1,957)=35.947$, $p<.001$). No significant differences were found for the dynamic friction settings. These results indicate that parameters for 'stiffness' and 'static friction' would be useful for inducing in a virtual haptic space subjective perceptions related to roughness and smoothness.

The next ANOVA examined the 'hard' and 'soft' subjective reports against the haptic virtual materials settings. The interaction between the two factors was found to be significant ($F(1,452)=13.231$, $p<.001$). An analysis of the simple main effect was conducted in each level of the parameters. In the stiffness condition, adjusted parameters were higher on the 'hard' condition compared to the 'soft' condition ($F(1,678)=28.667$, $p<.001$). No difference was found for the static friction condition and dynamic friction condition versus perceived hardness or softness. These results indicate that parameters for 'stiffness' would be useful for inducing subjective perceptions related to hardness and softness.

A third ANOVA was conducted to examine the reported sensations of 'elasticity' and 'inelasticity' with the haptic virtual materials setting. The interaction between the two factors was found to be significant, ($F(1,368)=5.24$, $p<.01$). Next, to investigate the differences of haptic sensations on each material setting, an analysis of the simple main effect was conducted. For the simple main effect, the settings were higher on the elastic condition compared to the inelastic condition in the stiffness condition ($F(1,552)=4.921$, $p<.05$). In the static friction condition, no difference was found. In the dynamic friction condition, adjusted parameters were higher on the elastic condition compared to the inelastic condition ($F(1,552)=5.251$, $p<.05$). These results indicate that parameters for 'stiffness' and 'dynamic friction' would affect subjective perceptions of elasticity. Although the exact causes of the elasticity-related reported sensations are not known, we speculate from these results that they are associated with the dynamic friction as it is experienced kinesthetically in the system of the arm and hand moving the stylus. Some of the elasticity may be from the actual physical properties of the joints and components and some may be from software idiosyncrasies. At the same time, much of this sensation of the elasticity is suspected to be an illusory, phantom sensation due to the conditions of the task and the visual perception of its virtual space. This sensation requires more and different experiments but, in keeping with the objective of this study, the responses associated with elasticity were not included in the data used in the following sections to model the perceptual space.

4 Discussion and Conclusions

The results described above generally corroborate those found in previous tactile studies of real-world objects, such as [3] and [5], which were, however, mainly focused on sensations from mechanoreceptors. Here, possible foundations for kinesthetic sensation models are proposed, based on the responses collected. Figure 4 shows clustering of hard and soft reports as plotted against the parameters used in the experiments. The asterisks in the legend indicate that these are aggregated hard and aggregated soft sets, formed by disregarding the "neither hard nor soft" responses and grouping all of each primitive together, ignoring modifiers (for example, Soft* includes "a little soft"). The figure demonstrates that sensations related to softness were less localized. It would be expected both intuitively and from the ANOVA results that stiffness coefficient plays a major role in hardness but the figure shows that the relationship is not straightforward. Figure 5, similarly, shows clusters of the combined rough and smooth reports. In this case, static friction coefficient would be expected to be the main parameter but the figure reveals, again, that simply increasing value of this coefficient will not necessarily result in a proportional increase in subjective sensations of roughness. These results demonstrate that more nuanced and nonlinear adjustments of multiple parameters are required to reliably communicate a specific sensation to the user.

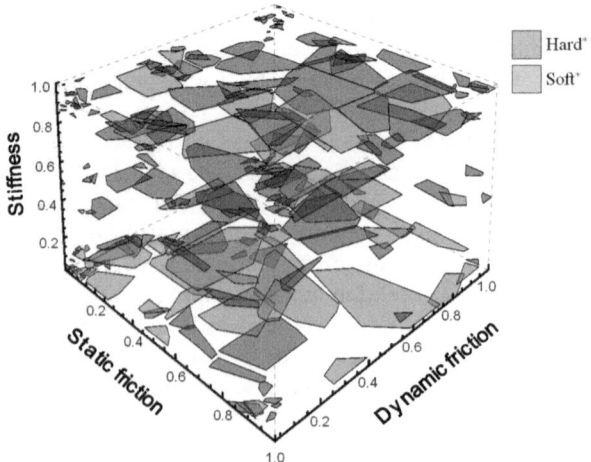

Fig. 4. Semantic characterization clusters plotted against haptic materials parameters shows that higher values of stiffness coefficient leading to perceived hardness (and, otherwise, lower stiffness to softness) is not rejected but also does not exhibit a straightforward, linear relationship

Fig. 6 shows each of the four basic surface sensations as it would be perceived at the setting expected to elicit the response. Fig. 6(I) models hardness as it was reported at high values of stiffness coefficient (and at various values of the other two parameters), Fig. 6(II) models softness as it was reported in low stiffness, Fig. 6(III) models roughness at high values of static friction coefficient, and Fig. 6(IV) models smoothness at low values of static friction coefficient. The generalizations shown were obtained through polynomial interpolation (of the third order) of the corresponding empirical densities over the whole range of the parameters. These models again demonstrate that system interface designers cannot simply rely on the physical meaning of the virtual haptic parameters to get the expected result. They will instead need to use more precise support and, due to the nonlinear and irregular nature of the perceptual space vis-à-vis the haptic materials coefficients, this design support should be incorporated as part of the interface design tools.

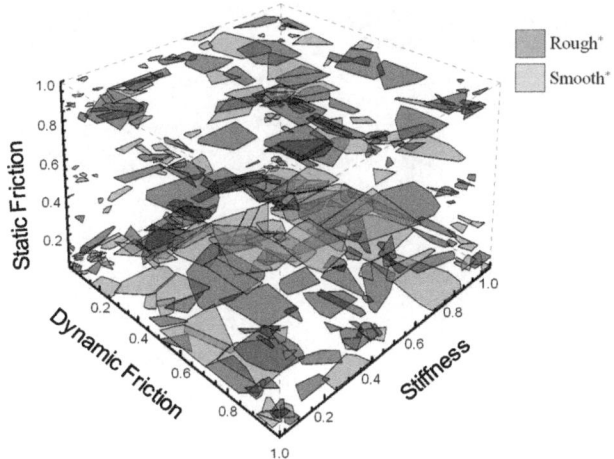

Fig. 5. Semantic characterization clusters plotted against haptic materials parameters shows higher static friction coefficient leading to perceived roughness (and lower static friction to softness) is not rejected but also does not exhibit a straightforward, linear relationship

The study described created a collection of open-ended verbal responses to specific haptic stimulus settings on the PHANToM Omni device in controlled, interview-based experiments. Moderators recorded the verbal responses as complete text entries and those entries were deconstructed by the Japanese morphological analysis tool MeCab. The decomposition resulted in adjective, verb, noun, and adverb terms thought to be related to the haptic sensations of interest in the experiments. These resulting terms were weighted by adverbial phrases and linked to the settings at which they were recorded. A correlation was detected which suggests that similar settings elicit similar responses in users with a relatively homogeneous cultural and linguistic background and that the sensations causing those responses can be modeled for practical application.

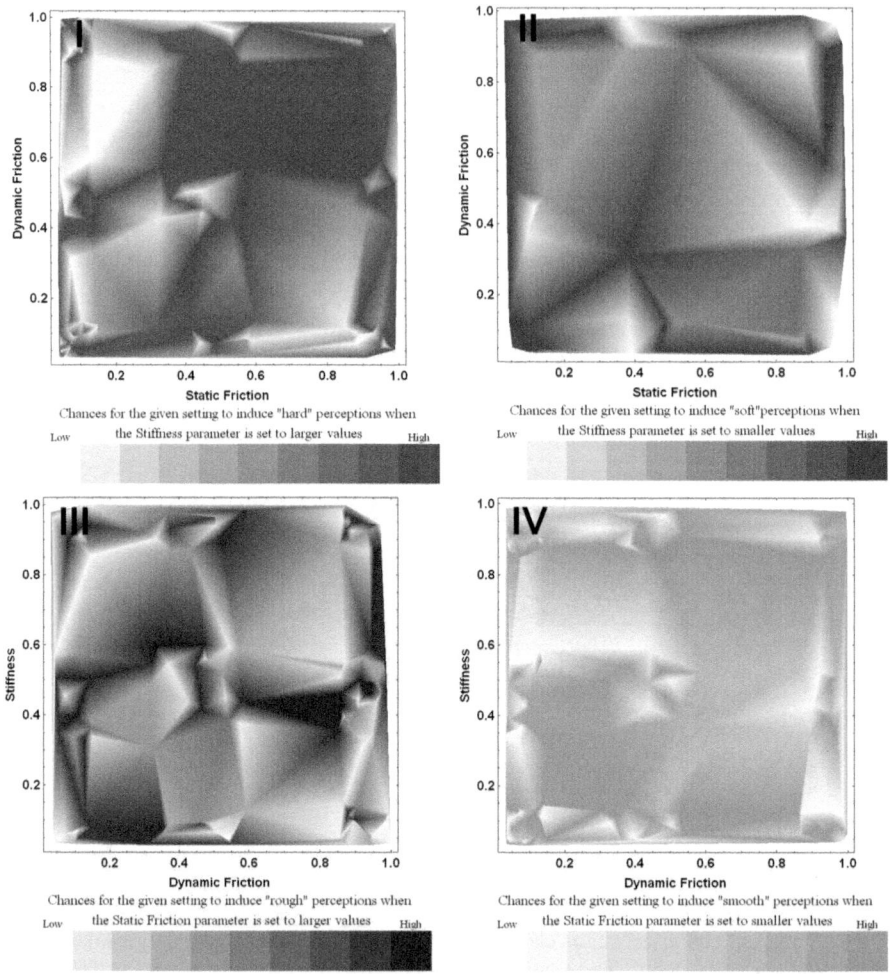

Fig. 6. Generalized modeling of the surface parameters against haptic perceptions suggests the space requires simultaneous and nonlinear manipulation of the given settings to possibly induce specific perceived haptic qualities in kinesthetically elicited haptic sensations (see text for details)

The most important finding in the results, adding to previous studies, is that the subjective response to parameter settings is not obvious from the semantic labels of the settings. Interface designers may reasonably expect, for example, that increasing values of the parameter associated, based on the underlying physical model, with the virtual stiffness would result in a direct and proportional increase in perceived hardness, or that decreasing values of the parameter associated with the virtual friction would lead to a similarly increased subjective smoothness. This study demonstrated that, while some of those basic expectations are not completely misguided, the relationship is neither linear nor robust. This finding has consequences both for the descriptive terms given to the software settings and for development of haptic interfaces that are constructed with those terms as guidelines. The presented study focused on a morphological analysis of three major categories of haptic sensation, which was sufficient for categorizing nine-tenths of the sessions. Other responses were reported and more extensive experimentation would allow a more detailed modeling of the categories analyzed, as well as adding to the number of "objective" categories, e.g. related to elasticity and "springiness" (see [3] for a relevant study).

References

1. Lederman, S.J., Klatzky, R.L.: Haptic perception: A tutorial, Atten. Percept. Psychophys. 71(7), 1439–1459 (2009)
2. Suga, M., Okamoto, T., Oshiro, M., Tsutsumi, N., Sakai, T.: Sensible human projects: haptic modeling and surgical simulation based on measurements of practical patients with MR elastography–measurement of elastic modulus. Stud. Health. Technol. Inform. 70, 334–340 (2000)
3. Hollins, M., Faldowski, R., Rao, S., Young, F.: Perceptual dimensions of tactile surface texture: a multidimensional scaling analysis. Percept. Psychophys. 54(6), 697–705 (1993)
4. Smith, A.M., Scott, S.H.: Subjective scaling of smooth surface friction. J. Neurophysiol. 75(5), 1957–1962 (1996)
5. Tiest, W., Kappers, A.: Analysis of haptic perception of materials by multidimensional scaling and physical measurements of roughness and compressibility. Acta Psychol. 121(1), 1–20 (2006)
6. MacLean, K., Enriquez, M.: Perceptual Design of Haptic Icons. In: Proc. of Eurohaptics, Dublin, Ireland (2003)
7. MacLean, K.: Haptic Interaction Design for Everyday Interfaces. E. Source: Reviews of Human Factors and Ergonomics 4, 149–194 (2008)
8. Cooper, E.W., Kryssanov, V.V., Ogawa, H.: Building a Framework for Communication of Emotional State through Interaction with Haptic Devices. In: Nordahl, R., Serafin, S., Fontana, F., Brewster, S. (eds.) HAID 2010. LNCS, vol. 6306, pp. 189–196. Springer, Heidelberg (2010)
9. Smith, J., MacLean, K.: Communicating Emotion Through a Haptic Link: Design Space and Methodology. J. of Human-Computer Studies 65(4), 376–387 (2007)
10. OpenHaptics Toolkit, Sensable, http://www.sensable.com/products-openhaptics-toolkit.htm (accessed May 2011)
11. Kudo, T.: MeCab: Yet Another Part-of-speech and Morphological Analyzer, http://mecab.sourceforge.net (accessed May 2011)
12. Den, Y., Nakamura, J., Ogiso, T., and Ogura, H.: A proper approach to Japanese morphological analysis: Dictionary, model, and evaluation. In: Proc. LREC, pp. 1019–1024 (2008)
13. Hasegawa, D., Rzepka, R., Araki, K.: Evaluation of Connectives Acquisition in a Humanoid Robot Using Direct Physical Feedback. In: Orgun, M.A., Thornton, J. (eds.) AI 2007. LNCS (LNAI), vol. 4830, pp. 664–668. Springer, Heidelberg (2007)

Analysis of the JND of Stiffness in Three Modes of Comparison

Umut Koçak, Karljohan Lundin Palmerius, Camilla Forsell,
Anders Ynnerman, and Matthew Cooper

C-Research, Linköping University, Sweden
{umut.kocak,karljohan.lundin.palmerius,camilla.forsell,anders.ynnerman,
matthew.cooper}@liu.se

Abstract. Understanding and explaining perception of touch is a non-trivial task. Even seemingly trivial differences in exploration may potentially have a significant impact on perception and levels of discrimination. In this study, we explore different aspects of contact related to stiffness perception and their effects on the just noticeable difference (JND) of stiffness are surveyed. An experiment has been performed on non-deformable, compliant objects in a virtual environment with three different types of contact: Discontinuous pressure, continuous pressure and continuous lateral motion. The result shows a significantly better discrimination performance in the case of continuous pressure (a special case of nonlinearity), which can be explained by the concept of haptic memory. Moreover, it is found that the perception is worse for the changes that occur along the lateral axis than the normal axis.

Keywords: Perception, stiffness, exploratory procedures, JND.

1 Introduction

Research in haptics has extensively grown in the last decade within different disciplines. In addition to improvements in hardware and software solutions, the way we, as human beings, perceive objects by the act of touching has also been under focus in the psychophysics branch. Understanding our perception mechanism as well as our limitations has the potential to guide the development of more effective haptic hardware and software solutions.

Various physical and geometrical properties of objects have been surveyed under the concept of perception. Perception of touch, however, is not easy to explain considering that several factors play a role in the process. The perception of an object is tightly bound to the nature of the contact, which may include one or more different exploratory procedures [5]. Static contact, lateral motion, contour following and pressure are among the various ways of touch providing different kinds of perception cues [5]. Some studies have proven that the choice of exploratory procedures has a significant effect on the perception of the object. For example, [4,12] showed that the type of sensory requirements for an optimal softness discrimination differ between exploring with a tool and exploring with fingers.

E.W. Cooper et al. (Eds.): HAID 2011, LNCS 6851, pp. 22–31, 2011.
© Springer-Verlag Berlin Heidelberg 2011

One of the most frequently surveyed material properties is stiffness (or compliance) since it refers to hardness/softness, which is one of the major components to understand the type of the material. Several studies have been conducted on just noticeable difference (JND) with different scenarios and ranges. The effects of exploratory procedures on stiffness perception, however, has not been shown as much interest. There are a few studies [2,4,12] surveying different aspects of contact on perception.

We suspect that understanding the effects of exploratory procedures on perception has the potential to affect our choices of exploration in real life by helping us choose better exploration techniques for different purposes. In this study, therefore, we explore the effects of some aspects of exploratory procedures on stiffness perception. We start by identifying and discussing different stiffness transitions which may occur in real situations such as surgery and clinical palpation. We explore whether touching continuously or discontinuously affects the stiffness discrimination. In the case of continuous contact, the discrimination of stiffness along lateral and normal axis are also compared. The unique aspect of the study is the comparison of the JNDs of stiffness for three different types of contact. The dependency of stiffness JND on the nature of the contact has been surveyed by an experiment performed with the subjects in a virtual environment. The results show that JND is significantly affected by the way we touch.

2   Related Work

Numerous perception studies have considered the various physical and geometrical properties of objects as well as the effects of different modalities and ways of grasping. Stiffness (or compliance) is one of the most studied properties, representing the hardness or softness of an object. The most common means to explore stiffness perception is to present a measure showing how well humans can perceive the varying levels of hardness or softness; to present this in the form of a JND. The results found vary depending on the differences between the methods employed. Effects of other factors such as multi-modality, cutaneous, kinaesthetic cues are also being surveyed.

There are a number of studies (e.g [14]) which have examined the JND in the stiffness. The effects of force and work cues on compliance discrimination were surveyed in [13] and the significant effect of force cues on discrimination was emphasized. In [15], the effect of surface deformation cues was examined and it was shown that the subjects' ability to discriminate the difference in stiffness was reduced by a factor of more than three without deformation cues.

The effect of visual information on stiffness perception was explored in the studies [11,16]. A dominance of visual feedback over kinaesthetic sense of hand position was demonstrated in [11]. Compliant objects that are further away were perceived to be softer in the case of haptic feedback alone [16], while the addition of the visual information reduced the bias.

Further studies [2,4,12] have examined the effects of exploratory procedures on stiffness perception. These exploratory procedures directly affect which properties of the object can be observed and how we perceive them. In [12], the contribution of tactile and kinaesthetic cues were explored for deformable and non-deformable objects. It was shown that the tactile information alone is sufficient for discrimination capacity of deformable objects while additional kinaesthetic feedback is necessary for non-deformable compliant objects. When a tool was used for exploration, additional kinaesthetic cues were found to be necessary for all types of objects [4]. Squeezing a deformable object between thumb and index finger was explored in [2,9]. Tactile information was found to be negligible for the scenario of squeezing objects between thumb and index finger [9]. These findings in the literature demonstrate the importance of the exploratory procedure in perception.

Some of the studies mentioned above explore different aspects of exploratory procedures but none of them compare the stiffness perception during different modes of transition, which we anticipate will be important in both real situations and computer simulated environments.

3   Modes of Transition

There are various ways of exploring an object including poking, contour following, squeezing, tapping with a tool, etc. Mainly the style of the motion, how we move our hands (or a tool), results in different exploratory techniques. If exploration is considered from the surface point of view, there are two principle directions: Normally directed and lateral motion. The movement along the normal direction refers to pushing into an object by applying a pressure, providing a sense of hardness [5]. The term "lateral motion" is mostly used for the exploration technique to obtain information about the texture of a surface [5], however we will consider the "lateral motion", as in [1], as the movements of the haptic device performed to perceive the topography of a surface like in the case of contour following. This type of lateral motion is common in real life situations such as palpation, surgical cuts, drawing or painting.

In addition to the direction of movement we also consider how the transition occurs between two different stiffnesses during comparison. One type would be comparison of two objects with different stiffnesses by separately touching the objects, which we call discontinuous contact. Another way of comparison is to discriminate a stiffness change during exploration without taking the probe away from the object. We call the latter one continuous the contact.

The combination of the two concepts of touch—continuity and the motion axis—creates different exploration scenarios as illustrated in figure 1. We aim to survey stiffness perception under these concepts by finding the JND of stiffness. The different conditions of the experiment are named depending on the type of contact.

DP-Discontinuous Pressure Comparison: In *Discontinuous Pressure Comparison* the contact refers to applying a pressure normal to the surface of an object and separately touching different objects in order to compare their hardness. In other words, the subject experiences a pause in the time domain between

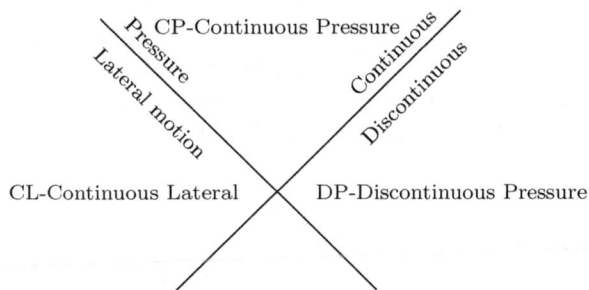

Fig. 1. Two aspects of contact during stiffness change: Continuity and Axis of Motion. The discontinuity during touch refers to touching discrete objects separately in order to discriminate the stiffness difference between them. While continuity corresponds to stiffness change during contact with the same object. The continuous stiffness change has been surveyed as two types: Lateral stiffness change and stiffness change along the surface normal axis during applied pressure, which is a special case of nonlinearity.

exploration of different stiffness values. This is the most common procedure followed in perception studies (e.g [12,4,11]).

CP-Continuous Pressure Comparison: When one is applying palpation to a surface, it is common in real life that the ratio of stress to strain changes with strain resulting in a stiffness that changes during contact. One can wonder how sensitive human beings are to these changes or whether we perceive or react differently than the previous condition (*Discontinuous Pressure (DP)*).

Similarly to visual memory, our minds can remember the perceived touch information for a limited period of time after a haptic exploration. The perceived information in the brain decays with time, which shows the limitation of the haptic memory. For instance in [10], the representation of object mass was found to be short-lived (two seconds). In the case of stiffness comparison, the interruption during discontinuous contact forces us to remember the pervious representation while touching an object. Discrimination of the changes during continuous contact has no such memory demand since the change occurs at a transition point during contact and perceiving the transition itself is sufficient for discrimination, instead of explicit comparison of stiffnesses. The case of *Continuous Pressure Comparison* can be thought of as detecting a transition instead of a memory task. Therefore it would be reasonable to expect better performance in the discrimination when the change occurs continuously allowing exploration without interruption.

In addition to the differences in the nature of *Continuous Pressure Comparison* and *Discontinuous Pressure Comparison*, the rarity of pure linear stiffnesses in real life scenarios also makes it interesting to survey the discrimination that occurs during palpation. Tumours underneath a tissue, bone structure under a fat layer, feeling veins during needle insertion are some cases with stiffness varying with strain. In addition, most soft tissues are also known to show nonlinear behaviour, but to the authors' knowledge there has been very little work on the perception of nonlinearity in stiffness. In [6] the perception of nonlinearity and in [8] the effects of shear and normal forces of nonlinear tissues on perception were explored. In neither of these studies, however, was the JND explored. In the *Continuous Pressure Comparison* condition we are surveying a special case of nonlinearity.

CL-Continuous Lateral Comparison: During *Continuous Lateral Comparison*, the stiffness is to be discriminated continuously but a change occurs with respect to lateral motion over the surface. This condition should not be confused with the use of lateral motion of fingers touching a texture for tactile information. The movement of the haptic device resembles contour following, possibly providing kinaesthetic cues, however, we include no contour change in our study, but instead, survey the discrimination of stiffness across a flat surface.

The concept of kinaesthetic height cues from varying stiffness over lateral motion was surveyed in [1]. Instead of the stiffness perception, Choi et al. focused on how hand movement is affected by the stiffness changes during lateral motion over the surface and came up with the force constancy theory. It was shown that during exploration of a virtual surface by a haptic probe, the user has a tendency to keep the applied force constant. This results in a change in the height of hand position due to a stiffness change during exploration of a flat surface. In our case of lateral motion, we are interested in perception of the stiffness changes, therefore visual cues about the height of hand position were eliminated during the experiment.

The fourth possible combination (Discontinuous-Lateral) describes discrimination between the stiffness of two separate objects under lateral motion with a pause between each palpation. This scenario is not considered in this survey since we see no important applications to real life situations.

4   Evaluation

To explore the effect of the three different contact types (hereafter referred to as conditions) on stiffness perception as described above, we performed an experiment. The following section describes the method applied.

4.1   Method

The experiment was performed in a virtual environment and a Desktop Phantom and a semi-transparent framework were used as the equipment, as illustrated in figure 2(a). Each stimulus was composed of three virtual boxes (providing force feedback depending on *Hooke's law*) that were visually rendered as in figure 2(b). The orientation of the boxes was adjusted such that the palpation occurs on the axis perpendicular to the desk. The boxes were not visually changing due to the compression and the haptic probe was rendered as a sphere which disappeared in the boxes during contact in all situations to prevent the visual cues about the strain applied. The subject was also prevented from seeing the real hand position

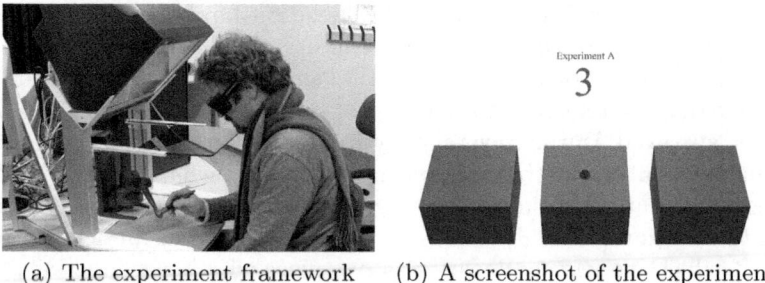

(a) The experiment framework   (b) A screenshot of the experiment

Fig. 2. (a) A 3D virtual image registered with the real hand position is obtained with the help of a semi-transparent mirror and stereo glasses. (b) The type of the experiment and the question number was rendered at the top of the view.

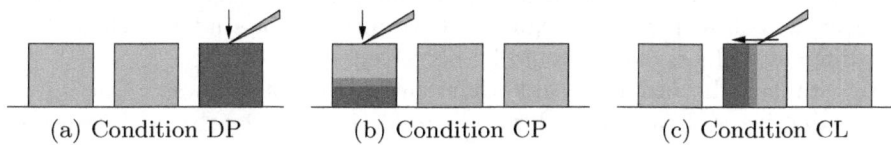

(a) Condition DP   (b) Condition CP   (c) Condition CL

Fig. 3. Three virtual boxes were presented to the subjects during each individual trial. The subjects were asked to find the single harder box among the three and the location of the harder box was randomized during the experiment. The way the harder box differed from the others depended on the type of the experiment. Interpolation is applied around the transition region in condition CP and CL to prevent an obvious discontinuity in stiffness.

under the semi-transparent mirror by setting the background color to bright white. In each individual trial the subjects were thus presented with three boxes. Two of the boxes were identical while one of them was harder in different ways depending on the specific condition, see description below. The force feedback from the boxes was evaluated by multiplying the stiffness and the depth of probe from the surface of the box, based on Hooke's Law.

Three different conditions were designed: DP, where the subjects were presented with three different boxes with linear stiffness, one of which was harder than the other two which had the reference stiffness, (figure 3(a)). The second condition, CP, included two boxes with reference stiffness and a third one which has a nonlinear stiffness as illustrated in figure 3(b). The nonlinearity was modelled as two piece-wise linear stiffnesses. The first linear region had the same stiffness as the other two boxes while the second linear region was always harder. In the third condition, CL, one of the three boxes had the reference stiffness on the right half while the left side was set to a harder stiffness, (figure 3(c)). The subjects were asked to make a lateral motion over the surface for CL and to apply a downward palpation for the other two conditions. The higher stiffness in each condition was changed depending on the subjects' responses, while the reference stiffness was kept constant. The relationship between the higher stiffness and the reference stiffness for each condition is illustrated in figure 4.

For all three conditions the height of the boxes were set to 3 cm. In the literature a wide range of reference stiffnesses, varying from 100 N/m to 16900 N/m [2], have been surveyed. During several pilot studies various stiffness values had been tried out. It was observed that the continuous use of the haptic device with higher stiffness values can result in overheating of the motors, requiring a break for the system to cool down. Finally, 100 N/m was determined as a reference stiffness.

In *CP*, which models nonlinearity as two piece-wise linear functions, the first linear region was active for strains less than 2 cm and the second for larger strains. In *CL* the subjects were told to make 'sweeping' movements sideways (left-to-right-to-left) across the surface. The horizontal position of the change was kept constant in the middle. In these two conditions which include a transition point, linear interpolation was applied across a neighbourhood of the transition point in order to prevent an obvious discontinuity. This interpolation region, however, was chosen small enough (0.5 cm) during pilot studies such that only two different stiffness values would be perceived.

To establish the just noticeable difference (JND) of stiffness a one-up two-down adaptive staircase procedure was used [7]. An adaptive staircase starts with an initial difference and, depending on an individual subject's responses, it changes the magnitude of the difference such that it converges to the perception limit of discrimination for that subject. In the case of a one-up two-down staircase, the magnitude is decreased following two consecutive correct responses and increased after each single incorrect response. This procedure converges to a stimulus level at which participants can make accurate responses with a certainty of 70.7%. In our case each session started with a stiffness difference of 20 N/m (20% of the reference stiffness value). Initially, the stiffness difference was changed by increments of 9 N/m and then by 4.5 N/m after the third reversal and by 2.25 N/m after the sixth reversal. A reversal occurred when the stiffness changed from increasing to decreasing, or vice versa. The session was

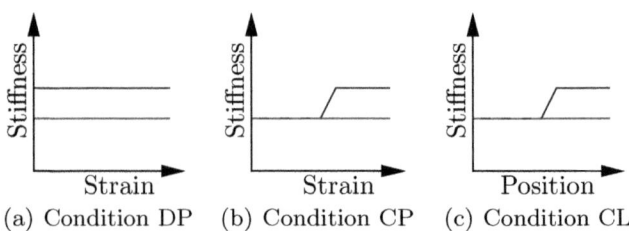

(a) Condition DP   (b) Condition CP   (c) Condition CL

Fig. 4. The stiffness changes for the conditions. The blue and red lines refer to the reference and the harder stiffnesses respectively. In condition DP, the act of touching for distinguishing between different levels of stiffness occurs discontinuously, while in condition CP and CL the subjects were to feel the difference during continuous contact. Interpolation results in a smoother change around the transition region for conditions CP and CL.

terminated after nine reversals and the average of the peaks and valleys of the last six reversals were calculated to be the JND.

Twelve subjects took part in the experiment, 10 male and 2 female. They were all undergraduate or graduate students aged between 27 and 40 years (mean age was 30). 8 of the subjects had tried a haptic device a few times previous to the experiment, 3 had used it quite often, and 1 had never tried it before. All subjects had normal or corrected to normal vision. They received no compensation for taking part in the experiment.

The evaluation was performed as a within-subjects design with one independent variable (stiffness) having three levels   (DP vs. CP vs. CL) or conditions. The experiment was performed over three separate sessions where each condition was carried out once. The presentation order of the conditions for each subject was balanced by using a Latin-square procedure. The placement of the harder box was randomized for each trial.

Before the experiment began background information was obtained from each subject. They then reviewed written instruction material and were instructed about the equipment and the tasks to be performed. Before each of the three separate sessions they also completed a set of practice trials. For each individual trial the task was to identify the harder box, out of the three, and give a response by pressing a button placed on the haptic device while pointing to that box. They were told to make a sweeping movement across the surface of the boxes for the CL session, to apply a downward palpation for the other two sessions. Total participation time lasted 30–40 minutes (including the introductory part).

5   Results

The values of each subject for all three conditions were analyzed for the 12 participants. Since the data deviated from normality according to the Kolmogorov-Smirnov and Shapiro-Wilks tests, non-parametric tests were used. A Friedman ANOVA by ranks with a decision criterion of 0.05 showed that there was a significant difference between the three conditions, Chi-Square (N=12 , df=2) = 12.667 p= 0.001.

To determine which conditions significantly differ, Wilcoxon signed-rank tests were used for post-hoc testing and a Bonferroni correction was applied meaning that all effects are reported at a 0.0167 (0.05/3) level of significance. There was a significant difference between condition DP and condition CP, Z=-3.061 p<0.001 and between CL and CP, z=-4.71 p=0.003 but no significant difference was observed between conditions DP and CL, Z=-2,746 p=0.677.

The analysis of the results shows that the discrimination performance due to nonlinearity of stiffness is much better than the other two conditions: the stiffness change along lateral motion and comparing objects with different stiffness. The mean value of the JND for the nonlinearity case (*Continuous Pressure*) is 5.23±3.01%, while the *Discontinuous Pressure* and *Continuous Lateral* contacts have a mean JND of 12.91±6.93% and 15.77±9.59% respectively.

6   Discussion and Conclusions

The aim of the study was to compare the stiffness discrimination for different scenarios representing different exploration techniques. Some studies [2,4,5,12] and the variance of the results of JND studies support that the perception is not trivial to explain and is affected by several factors including the exploratory procedure. Creating a scenario including all factors affecting perception is a challenging task, however we performed an experiment considering two aspects of touch: continuity and the axis of motion.

An experiment was performed to find the JND of stiffness for three different scenarios of contact: *Discontinuous pressure*, *Continuous pressure* (nonlinearity) and *Continuous lateral*. Instead of comparing the numerical JND values one by one with previous perception studies, we compared the JND performances between these different types of contact. Our main reasoning being that the studies [2,4,5,12] support the idea that perception is affected by several factors, therefore the numerical values depend on the experiment design. The comparison between the three contact scenarios shows that the discrimination performance is significantly better for the nonlinearity case than the others.

The significant difference between the results of *Continuous Pressure* and *Discontinuous Pressure* was expected due to the concept of haptic memory: the reason for the difference between the JNDs then being the interruption between exploring different stiffnesses. One interesting fact, however, is the substantial difference between the *Continuous Pressure* and *Continuous Lateral* showing the effect of the motion axis on discrimination, which brings us to the second outcome of the study: better discrimination along normal axis than lateral axis.

The only difference between the conditions *Continuous Pressure* and *Continuous Lateral* is that the stiffness change occurs along a different axis. A possible reason for a worse discrimination along the lateral axis might be the *force constancy* principle [1] which states that a user will subconsciously absorb changes in the normal directed force during lateral surface exploration.

The choice of exploratory procedures is related to the aim of the exploration and the type of object. In addition to quantification of our sensitivity to force and stiffness, it is also important to understand how it is affected by the exploratory procedures we choose. This knowledge has the potential to affect our choices of exploration in real life. For instance, the scenarios surveyed in this study, contact including nonlinearity and lateral motion is commonly observed in some medical procedures such as diagnosing a tumour, surgery, needle insertions etc. Knowing our limitations for different types of exploration could help us choose better exploration techniques for different aims. The limitation of our study is the difference between the tested and real life scenarios. For instance, observing nonlinearity in the form of two piecewise linear functions in real life is not so common. The significant results, however, are promising to continue exploring the topic with more realistic scenarios.

References

1. Choi, S., Walker, L., Tan, H.Z., Crittenden, S., Reifenberger, R.: Force constancy and its effect on haptic perception of virtual surfaces. ACM Transactions on Applied Perception 2(2), 89–105 (2005)
2. Freyberger, F.K., Färber, B.: Compliance discrimination of deformable objects by squeezing with one and two fingers. In: Eurohaptics 2006, pp. 271–276 (2006)
3. Jones, L.A., Hunter, I.W.: A perceptual analysis of stiffness. Experimental Brain Research 79(1), 150–156 (1990)
4. Lamotte, R.H.: Softness discrimination with a tool. The Journal of Neurophysiology 83(4), 1777–1786 (2000)
5. Lederman, S., Klatzky, R.: Haptic perception: A tutorial. Attention, Perception, and Psychophysics 71(7), 1439–1459 (2009)
6. Leib, R., Nisky, I., Karniel, A.: Perception of stiffness during interaction with delay-like nonlinear force field. In: Kappers, A.M.L., van Erp, J.B.F., Bergmann Tiest, W.M., van der Helm, F.C.T. (eds.) EuroHaptics 2010. LNCS, vol. 6191, pp. 87–92. Springer, Heidelberg (2010)
7. Levitt, H.: Transformed up-down methods in psychoacoustics. Journal of Acoustical Society of America 49, 467–477 (1971)
8. Misra, S., Fuernstahl, P., Ramesh, K., Okamura, A.M., Harders, M.: Quantifying perception of nonlinear elastic tissue models using multidimensional scaling. In: Worldhaptics 2009, pp. 570–575 (2009)
9. Roland, P., Ladegaard-Pedersen, H.: A quantitative analysis of sensations of tension and of kinasthesia in man: Evidence for a peripherally originating muscular sense and for a sense of effort. Brain 100(4), 671–692 (1977)
10. Shih, R., Dubrowski, A., Carnahan, H.: Evidence for haptic memory. In: World-Haptics 2009, pp. 145–149 (2009)
11. Srinivasan, M.A., Beauregard, G., Brock, D.: The impact of visual information on the haptic perception of stiffness in virtual environments. In: ASME Dynamic Systems and Control Division, pp. 555–559 (1996)
12. Srinivasan, M.A., Lamotte, R.H.: Tactual discrimination of softness. The Journal of Neurophysiology 73(1), 88–101 (1995)
13. Tan, H.Z., Durlach, N.I., Beauregard, G., Srinivasan, M.A.: Manual discrimination of compliance using active pinch grasp: The roles of force and work cues. Perception and Psychophysics 57(4), 495–510 (1995)
14. Tan, H.Z., Pang, X.-D., Durlach, N.I.: Manual resolution of length, force and compliance. In: ASME Dynamic Systems and Control Division, pp. 13–18 (1992)
15. Tiest, W.M.B., Kappers, A.M.: Cues for haptic perception of compliance. IEEE Transactions on Haptics 2(4), 189–199 (2009)
16. Wu, W.-C., Basdogan, C., Srinivasan, M.A.: Visual, haptic, and biomodal perception of size and stiffness in virtual environments. In: ASME Dynamic Systems and Control Division, pp. 19–26 (1999)

Models of and Experiments with Reaching Tasks in Haptic Virtual Environments

Mikhail Svinin[1] and Igor Goncharenko[2]

[1] Mechanical Engineering Department, Faculty of Engineering,
Kyushu University, 744 Motooka, Nishi-ku, Fukuoka 819-0395, Japan
`svinin@mech.kyushu-u.ac.jp`
[2] 3D System Division, I-Net Corporation, 13F, Nissay Aroma Square,
5-37-1 Kamata, Oota-ku, Tokyo 144-8721, Japan
`goncharenko@inet.co.jp`

Abstract. The paper presents an analysis of human reaching movements in manipulation of flexible objects. To predict the trajectory of human hand we resort to two models, the lowest polynomial order model for the hand movement and the minimum hand jerk model. First, we derive analytical solutions for these models for the dynamic environment represented by a multi-mass linear flexible object. Then, we present experimental results obtained with the use of a haptic interface. It is shown that the lowest polynomial order model does not fit with the experimental data while the prediction by the minimum hand jerk criterion matches the experimental patterns with reasonable accuracy.

Keywords: Human movements, reaching task, dynamic environment, modeling, haptic interface

1 Introduction

Understanding the trajectory formation in human reaching movements is a very important research problem in computational neuroscience and modern robotics. The problem can be attacked from different directions. One of the research lines deals with the sensory-motor feedback control and looks for a natural resolution of the redundancy of human movements [1]. Another, complimentary research line deals with the open-loop control and employs optimization approaches [5].

In this paper we will deal with the feedforward component of reaching movements and model it via optimization theory. In this approach, the trajectory of the human arm is predicted by minimizing, over the movement time T, an integral performance index $\mathcal{J}$ subject to boundary conditions imposed on start and end points. It is well established that for the unconstrained reaching movements the trajectory of human hand can be predicted with reasonable accuracy by the minimum hand jerk criterion [4]. Another popular model is based on the minimum joint torque change criterion [9].

While the above criteria captures well basic features of reaching movements in the free space, it remains to be seen if they are applicable to modeling of reaching

E.W. Cooper et al. (Eds.): HAID 2011, LNCS 6851, pp. 32–41, 2011.

movements in dynamic environments. A simple but not trivial example of reaching in a dynamic environment is the rest-to-rest manipulation of a linear chain of flexible objects with compensation of structural vibration. Despite seeming simplicity, this task requires a lot of skill that must be acquired by practicing. An interesting feature of this task, established in [3] for a single-spring flexible object, is that human controls the object in a very non-trivial way, keeping two distinct phases in the hand velocity profile.

One of the simplest control strategies is to specify the motion of the most distal link of the flexible object by the lowest-order polynomial satisfying the system boundary conditions. This control strategy was successfully verified for movements with a one-mass flexible object [3]. However, as shown in [8], it does not work well for multi-mass flexible objects. Another control strategy is to use the lowest-order polynomial for the specification of the motion of the foremost link of the system (that is the hand movement). In this paper we analyze the latter control strategy and compare it with the one based on the minimum had jerk model. Our theoretical and experimental analysis show that the minimum hand jerk model is a more consistent candidate for the prediction of reaching movements in the manipulation of flexible objects.

The paper is organized as follows. In Section 2, we introduce a mathematical model of the flexible object and derive analytical solutions for the lowest-order-polynomial model and for the minimum hand jerk model. These solutions are tested against experimental data in Section 3. Finally, conclusions are summarized in Section 4.

2   Reaching Movements in Dynamic Environments

In this section we consider reaching movements in a dynamic environment that is modeled as a multi-mass flexible object. First, we construct a mathematical model of the object and formulate a reaching task. Then we proceed to an analysis of two models for motion planning, the lowest order polynomial model and the minimum hand jerk model.

2.1   Multi-mass Flexible Object

Consider a chain system of n masses connected by n springs as shown in Fig. 1. The dynamic equations read

$$m_i \ddot{x}_i + k_i(x_i - x_{i-1}) + k_{i+1}(x_i - x_{i+1}) = 0, \tag{1}$$

$$m_n \ddot{x}_n + k_n(x_n - x_{n-1}) = 0, \tag{2}$$

where $i = 1, \ldots, n - 1$. Define the hand position $x_h \triangleq x_0$ and the object endpoint position $x_o \triangleq x_n$. Assume that the object is composed of the masses $m_i = m_o/n$, $i = 1, \ldots, n$, where m_o is the total mass of the flexible object. Also assume that all stiffness coefficients are equal and assign the stiffness distribution

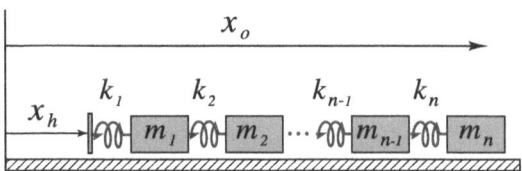

Fig. 1. Multi-mass object

from the condition that the n-mass system is statically equivalent[1] to a virtual one mass flexible system (of mass m_o and stiffness k_o), which gives $k_i = k_o\, n$, $i = 1, \ldots, n$.

For the symmetric mass and stiffness distribution the object dynamics (1,2) can be rearranged as

$$x_{i-1} = \frac{1}{(n\omega)^2}\, \ddot{x}_i + 2x_i - x_{i+1}, \quad i = 1, \ldots, n-1, \tag{3}$$

$$x_{n-1} = \frac{1}{(n\omega)^2}\, \ddot{x}_n + x_n, \tag{4}$$

where $\omega = \sqrt{k_o/m_o}$. The hand position $x_h \triangleq x_0$ can be expressed in terms of the object coordinate $x_o \triangleq x_n$ and its derivatives. Solving equations (3,4) recurrently for $i = n-1, n-2, \ldots, 0$, one obtains

$$x_h(t) = \sum_{l=0}^{n} \frac{C_{n+l}^{n-l}}{(n\omega)^{2l}}\, x_o^{(2l)}(t), \tag{5}$$

where $C_p^q = p!/(q!(p-q)!)$ denotes the binomial coefficients.

2.2   Reaching Task and the Boundary Conditions

Assume that a human subject is requested to make a reaching movement of length L and time T and stop the hand and all the masses of the object without excitation of oscillations. In other words, the subject is requested to generate a rest-to-rest motion command that eliminates residual vibrations. Without loss of generality we assume that the subject transports the masses from the initial state

$$x_i(0) = 0, \ \dot{x}_i(0) = 0, \quad i = 1, \ldots, n, \tag{6}$$

to the final state

$$x_i(T) = L, \ \dot{x}_i(T) = 0, \quad i = 1, \ldots, n. \tag{7}$$

---

[1] for the n-mass system under consideration and for the virtual one mass flexible system.

Assuming that the hand is at rest in the beginning and in the end of movement, one defines the boundary conditions

$$x_h(0) = 0, \quad \dot{x}_h(0) = 0, \quad \ddot{x}_h(0) = 0, \tag{8}$$

$$x_h(T) = L, \quad \dot{x}_h(T) = 0, \quad \ddot{x}_h(T) = 0. \tag{9}$$

In what follows, we will represent optimization problems in terms of the object end position $x_o \triangleq x_n$ that is the coordinate of the most distal mass. For this purpose we need to formulate the boundary conditions for x_o which can be obtained from the boundary conditions (6,7) and (8,8). Differentiating equations (3,4) sequentially, i-th equation $2i$ times, and considering them at $t = 0$ and $t = T$ one obtains $x_i^{(2)}(0) = x_i^{(3)}(0) = \ldots = x_i^{(2i+2)}(0) = 0$, and $x_i^{(2)}(T) = x_i^{(3)}(T) = \ldots = x_i^{(2i+2)}(T) = 0$. For $i = n$ one thus obtains the following boundary conditions for the object end position:

$$x_o(0) = 0, \quad \dot{x}_o(0) = \ldots = x_o^{(2n+2)}(0) = 0, \tag{10}$$

$$x_o(T) = L, \quad \dot{x}_o(T) = \ldots = x_o^{(2n+2)}(T) = 0. \tag{11}$$

2.3   Minimum Order Polynomial Model

One way to plan the reaching movements under consideration is to specify the motion of the most distal link $x_o(t)$ in the form of the lowest order polynomial satisfying the boundary conditions (10,11). This approach to the modeling of reaching movements with flexible objects was successfully verified for movements with a one-mass flexible object [3]. However, as shown in [8], it does not work well for multi-mass flexible objects.

In this section we analyze another method for the generation of human-like reaching movements where the lowest polynomial order model is used to specify the motion of the foremost link of the system, that is the hand motion. Interestingly, this method can be connected to the recently proposed definition of natural movements based on the Hamilton principle of analytical mechanics [7]. In what follows, we briefly review the Hamilton principle-based method [7] and apply it to the analysis of reaching movements in the manipulation of multi-mass flexible objects.

In analytical mechanics a system is called natural if it admits a potential function $\mathcal{V}(\boldsymbol{q}, \dot{\boldsymbol{q}})$ [6,2], where $\boldsymbol{q} \in \Re^n$ is the vector of generalized coordinates of the system. Natural systems satisfy Hamilton's principle, $\delta \int_0^T \mathcal{L}(\boldsymbol{q}, \dot{\boldsymbol{q}})\, dt = 0$, where $\mathcal{L} = \mathcal{K} - \mathcal{V}$, $\mathcal{K}$ is the kinetic energy of the system. The motion equations for the natural systems have the following form

$$\frac{d}{dt}\left(\frac{\partial \mathcal{L}}{\partial \dot{\boldsymbol{q}}}\right) - \frac{\partial \mathcal{L}}{\partial \boldsymbol{q}} = 0, \tag{12}$$

If there are non-conservative forces there takes place the extended Hamilton principle $\int_0^T (\delta \mathcal{L} - \delta \mathcal{W})\, dt = 0$, where $\delta \mathcal{W} = \delta \boldsymbol{q}^{\mathsf{T}} \boldsymbol{u}$ is the virtual work of the non-conservative forces $\boldsymbol{u}$. The motion equations are then set in the familiar form

$$\frac{d}{dt}\left(\frac{\partial \mathcal{L}}{\partial \dot{\boldsymbol{q}}}\right) - \frac{\partial \mathcal{L}}{\partial \boldsymbol{q}} = \boldsymbol{u}. \tag{13}$$

Note that the extended Hamilton principle is not variational because one cannot set δ in front of the integral. Also note that the Hamilton principle is a tool for the derivation of motion equations. It does not say anything about the solution as it obviously depends on the specific control $\boldsymbol{u}$. What is interesting in [7] is that the authors show how this principle and the related concept of natural systems can be used to formally define a solution of motion equations that can be called a natural reaching movement. The definition of this movement is based on the following coordinate transformation

$$\boldsymbol{\varphi}^{(k)} = \boldsymbol{q}. \tag{14}$$

This is a differential transformation from the original coordinates $\boldsymbol{q}$ to the new coordinates $\boldsymbol{\varphi}$. Therefore, it brings new integration constants that have to be selected to satisfy the boundary conditions of the reaching task:

$$\boldsymbol{q}(0) = \boldsymbol{q}_0, \quad \dot{\boldsymbol{q}}(0) = \dot{\boldsymbol{q}}_0, \quad \ddot{\boldsymbol{q}}(0) = \ddot{\boldsymbol{q}}_0, \dots, \boldsymbol{q}^{(l)}(0) = \boldsymbol{q}_0^{(l)}, \tag{15}$$

$$\boldsymbol{q}(T) = \boldsymbol{q}_T, \dot{\boldsymbol{q}}(T) = \dot{\boldsymbol{q}}_T, \ddot{\boldsymbol{q}}(T) = \ddot{\boldsymbol{q}}_T, \dots, \boldsymbol{q}^{(l)}(T) = \boldsymbol{q}_T^{(l)}. \tag{16}$$

In the new coordinates φ the Hamilton principle takes the following form

$$\delta \int_0^T L(\boldsymbol{\varphi}^{(k)}, \boldsymbol{\varphi}^{(k+1)}) \, dt = 0, \tag{17}$$

and, as shown in [7], it is satisfied if we set

$$\boldsymbol{u}^{(k)} = \boldsymbol{0}. \tag{18}$$

This is a formal definition of the potential forces in the new coordinates φ. It is to be noted that the same force $\boldsymbol{u}$ is non-conservative with respect to the original coordinates $\boldsymbol{q}$, while it is conservative with respect to the new coordinates φ. This definition may sound somewhat artificial but it can be a paradigm for the definition of natural reaching movements.

The solution to the differential equation (18) is obviously a polynomial with nk coefficients (integration constants). Note that the total number of the boundary conditions in (15,16) is $2n(l+1)$, and the motion equations (13) presume $2n$ integration constants. The numbers of integration constant are balanced if $nk = 2n(l+1) - 2n$. Therefore, one has to set $k = 2l$. Then, the trajectory of the natural reaching movement is defined by solving motion equations (13) with the control (18) under the boundary conditions (15,16). It was shown [7] under simulation that the lowest order polynomial model defined as above can capture the invariant features of reaching movements (rough straitness of the hand path and the bell-shaped hand velocity profile) in free space.

The natural reaching movement in [7] is defined for the force-driven systems for the case when $\dim \boldsymbol{q} = \dim \boldsymbol{u}$ (fully actuated systems). However, the same reasoning—setting the control input in the form of the lowest order polynomial—can be applied also for underactuated controllable systems that are driven kinematically. In our model of the multi-mass flexible object (1,2) the control is the hand position x_h. The object dynamics are given by (5). For $x_h = 0$ this equation has $2n$ integration constants. The total number of the boundary conditions (10,11) is $2(2n+3)$. Therefore, the differential equation for the control x_h should have the order $2(2n+3) - 2n = 2n + 6$, $x_h^{(2n+6)} = 0$, and, therefore,

$$x_h = \sum_{i=0}^{2n+5} \hat{\alpha}_i t^i. \tag{19}$$

Here, $\hat{\alpha}_i$ are the unknown coefficients to be determined. Under the specified control $x_h(t)$ (19) the object position is established as

$$x_o = \sum_{i=0}^{2n+5} \bar{\alpha}_i t^i + \sum_{i=1}^{n} \bar{\beta}_{1i} \sin p_i t + \bar{\beta}_{2i} \cos p_i t. \tag{20}$$

where

$$p_k = 2\omega n \cos \frac{(n-k+1)\pi}{2n+1}, \quad k = 1, 2, \dots, n. \tag{21}$$

are the natural frequencies of the object, obtained from the system (1,2) with x_h set to zero [8]. The coefficients $\bar{\alpha}_i, \bar{\beta}_{1i}, \bar{\beta}_{2i}$ in (20) are found from the boundary conditions (10,11). Having defined them, one can finally obtain

$$\hat{\alpha}_i = \sum_{l=0}^{n} \frac{C_{n+l}^{n-l}}{(n\omega)^{2l}} A_{2l+i}^{2l} \bar{\alpha}_{2l+i}, \quad i = 0, 1, \dots, 2n+5, \tag{22}$$

where $A_i^k = i!/(i-k)!$ are the permutation numbers, and the summation is conducted for the indexes l and i such that $2l + i \leq 2n + 5$.

2.4   Minimum Hand Jerk Model

Consider now a minimum hand jerk model where the criterion of optimality is defined as

$$J = \frac{1}{2} \int_0^T \left(\frac{d^3 x_h}{dt^3} \right)^2 dt. \tag{23}$$

Differentiating the hand position (5) three times and substituting the result into (23), one can represent the minimum hand jerk criterion in the following form:

$$J = \frac{1}{2} \int_0^T \left(\sum_{l=0}^{n} \frac{C_{n+l}^{n-l}}{(n\omega)^{2l}} x_o^{(2l+3)} \right)^2 dt. \tag{24}$$

The object trajectory $x_o(t)$ minimizing criterion (24) under the boundary conditions (10,11) must satisfy the following Euler-Lagrange equation

$$\sum_{s=0}^{n} \sum_{l=0}^{n} \frac{C_{n+s}^{n-s} C_{n+l}^{n-l}}{(n\omega)^{2s} (n\omega)^{2l}} x_o^{(2\{l+s+3\})} = 0. \tag{25}$$

It is easy to show that the characteristic equation corresponding to (25) has 6 zero roots and $2n$ pairs of imaginary roots $\pm\imath p_s$, where p_s, $s = 1, 2, \ldots, n$, are the natural frequencies of the object defined by (21). The optimal object trajectory is therefore defined as

$$x_o(t) = \sum_{i=0}^{5} \alpha_i\, t^i + \sum_{i=1}^{n} (\beta_{1i} + \beta_{2i}t)\sin p_i t + (\beta_{3i} + \beta_{4i}t)\cos p_i t, \tag{26}$$

where α_i and β_{ji} are the constant coefficients. For any fixed n, $T > 0$ and $\omega \neq 0$ these coefficients are defined uniquely from the boundary conditions (10,11).

3   Experimental Results

To check the velocity profiles of reaching movements with multi-mass objects, we conducted an experiment. In the experimental setup, shown in Fig. 2, a haptic device (PHANToM Premium 151A/3DOF, maximum exertable force 8.5N) is connected to computer (dual core CPU, Intel Pentium 4, 3.0 GHz) through PCI interface.

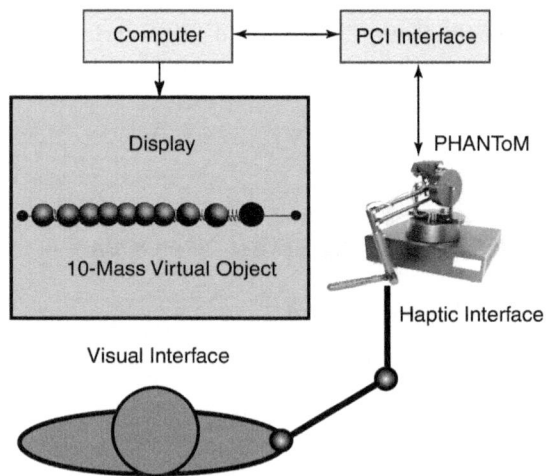

Fig. 2. Experimental setup

Five right-handed naïve subjects (males, aged between 25 and 35 years old) participated in the experiments. The subjects were instructed to move a multi-mass virtual flexible object, with the 1st mass (shown in black color in Fig. 2) "connected" to human hand by haptic feedback generated by the PHANToM motors. The hand & object system was at rest at the start point. Before starting the movement the subject positioned the PHANToM pointer to the 1st mass and "connected" it to the hand by pressing a button on the computer keyboard.

The subjects were requested to move the flexible object and stop the hand and all the masses at a target point. The subjects made these rest-to-rest movements along a line (in the direction from left to right) in the horizontal plane using the PHANToM stylus. The one-dimensional movements were implemented in software by setting a higher constraint force in the direction orthogonal to the movement line. The positions of the hand and the object were displayed on the computer monitor, providing the subject with real-time visual feedback. The object dynamics were simulated in the computer (4th-order Runge-Kutta method with constant step $h = 0.001$s) and real-time haptic feedback was supplied to the subject through the PHANToM stylus. The hand position and velocity were measured by the PHANToM hardware.

As the reaching movements under consideration are quite unusual and different from what we experience in daily life, the experiment was conducted in three days. On the preliminary day we conducted a general evaluation of the subjects' performance. The subjects familiarized with the experimental setup, comprehended the reaching task, performed movement trials and learned the unusual dynamic environment. The subjects were requested to produce reaching movements in a natural way, on their own pace, trading off the speed and the comfortability. A trial was considered to be successful if the task was completed within certain position, and velocity tolerances. The subject was given an audio feedback, generated by the computer, if a trial was successful. No data were recorded during the preliminary evaluation as the main purpose was to select such parameters of the movement task that would guarantee an acceptable rate of the successful trials and facilitate the learning process.

In the course of the preliminary evaluation, we selected the parameters of the object (the total mass $m_o = 3$kg, stiffness $k_o = 10$N/m, and the number of masses $n = 10$). For the experimental analysis we selected the reaching task with the traveling distance $L = 0.2$m, the movement time $T = 2.35$s, and the time tolerance $\Delta T = \pm 0.4$s. For each mass of the object we selected the following position, velocity, and acceleration tolerances to be satisfied at the start and end points: $\Delta x = \pm 0.012$m, $\Delta v = \pm 0.024$m/s, $\Delta a = \pm 0.16$m/s^2. For the hand, the start and end point position and velocity tolerances were set as $\Delta x = \pm 0.012$m, $\Delta v = \pm 0.05$m/s. A movement trial now was defined as successful if the subject was able to complete the reaching task within the above-specified tolerances.

Having selected the parameters of the reaching task, we proceeded further and conducted experiments in two days. On the 1st day the subjects performed the reaching task and completed 600 trials. The subject was given an audio feedback, generated by the computer, if a trial was successful. The experiment was conducted in two blocks. Upon completing 300 trials the subjects rested for about 30 minutes. The overall success rate achieved on the 1st day of the experiment is shown in Table 1. On the 2nd day (recording phase) the experiment was repeated in the similar manner. The data regarding the position and the velocity of the hand and those of the simulated masses were collected for analysis. These data were recorded at 100 Hz.

Table 1. Progress in motor training (success rate)

Subject	Day 1 (600 trials)	Day 2 (600 trials)	Total
Subject 1	54 (9.00%)	68 (11.33%)	122 (10.17%)
Subject 2	68 (11.33%)	94 (15.67%)	162 (13.50%)
Subject 3	84 (14.00%)	89 (14.83%)	173 (14.41%)
Subject 4	80 (13.33%)	96 (16.00%)	176 (14.67%)
Subject 5	100 (16.67%)	119 (19.83%)	219 (18.25%)

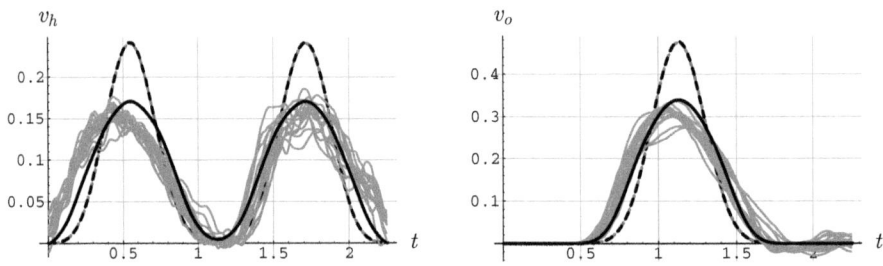

Fig. 3. Theoretical hand (left) and object (right) velocity profiles in comparison with experimental data (gray lines) of the first subject

As can be seen from Table 1, in the 2nd day of the experiment the success rate slightly increased for all the subjects in all the reaching tasks. This confirms the recovery and the increase of the motor memory. The resulting success rate is still far from perfect after two days of practicing. The relatively low success rate can be explained by the complexity of the reaching task which features a sport-like movement. The behavior of the flexible object in this movement is non-trivial, which requires from the subject a good coordination skill. It was observed that in the successful trials the subjects produced the following movement strategy. In the beginning, the positions of all the masses coincide at the start point. During the first half of the movement the first (driving) mass, shown as black sphere in Fig. 2, is ahead of the last (most distal) mass, with the distance between the first and last masses being about 5cm. During the second half of the movement the configuration is reversed symmetrically. The driving mass becomes behind the last mass, and finally all the masses reach the target point.

Examination of the hand and object velocity profiles demonstrated that for all the subjects the experimental data were in favor of the minimum hand jerk model. Qualitatively, the resulting velocity patterns for all the subjects were similar. For the graphical illustration of the velocity profiles, we take the data of last 15 successful trials of the first subject and compare them with the theoretical predictions. To compare motions of different durations, the velocity profiles are time scaled using the average time of successful trials, $T = 2.259$s. The experimental velocity profiles are shown in Fig. 3 in gray color. The hand and object velocity profiles, predicted by the minimum hand jerk model, are shown in solid lines in Fig. 3. The predictions by lowest polynomial order model are shown there in dashed lines. As can be seen from Fig. 3, the collected experimental data are clearly in favor of the minimum hand jerk model.

4 Conclusions

An analysis of reaching movements in the manipulation of flexible objects has been undertaken in this paper. To predict the trajectory of the human hand, we have analyzed two models, the lowest polynomial order model and the minimum hand jerk model. Optimal solutions for these models have been established in the analytical form for the general case of n-mass linear flexible object. The solutions have been tested against experimental data obtained using a haptic interface. It has been demonstrated that the lowest polynomial order model does not fit with the experimental data while the prediction by the minimum hand jerk criterion matches the experimental patterns with reasonable accuracy.

References

1. Arimoto, S., Sekimoto, M., Hashiguchi, H., Ozawa, R.: Natural resolution of ill-posedness of inverse kinematics for redundant robots: A challenge to Bernstein's degrees-of-freedom problem. Advanced Robotics 19(4), 401–434 (2005)
2. Arnold, V.: Mathematical Methods of Classical Mechanics. Springer, Berlin (1980)
3. Dingwell, J., Mah, C., Mussa-Ivaldi, F.: Experimentally confirmed mathematical model for human control of a non-rigid object. Journal of Neurophysiology 91, 1158–1170 (2004)
4. Flash, T., Hogan, N.: The coordination of arm movements: An experimentally confirmed mathematical model. The Journal of Neuroscience 5(7), 1688–1703 (1985)
5. Flash, T., Hogan, N., Richardson, M.: Optimization principles in motor control. In: Arbib, M. (ed.) The Handbook of Brain Theory and Neural Networks, 2nd edn., pp. 827–831. MIT Press, Cambridge (2003)
6. Gantmacher, F.: Lectures in Analytical Mechanics. Mir Publishers, Moscow (1975)
7. Morita, S., Ohtsuka, T.: Natural motion trajectory generation based on Hamilton's principle. Transactions of the Society of Instrument and Control Engineers 42(1), 1–10 (2006) (in Japanese)
8. Svinin, M., Goncharenko, I., Luo, Z., Hosoe, S.: Reaching movements in dynamic environments: How do we move flexible objects? IEEE Transactions on Robotics 22(4), 724–739 (2006)
9. Uno, Y., Kawato, M., Suzuki, R.: Formation and control of optimal trajectory in human multijoint arm movement. minimum torque-change model. Biological Cybernetics 61, 89–101 (1989)

Consonance Perception of Vibrotactile Chords: A Feasibility Study

Yongjae Yoo, Inwook Hwang, and Seungmoon Choi

Haptics and Virtual Reality Laboratory
Department of Computer Science and Engineering
Pohang University of Science and Technology (POSTECH)
Republic of Korea
{dreamseed,inux,choism}@postech.ac.kr

Abstract. This paper is concerned with the perception of complex vibrotactile stimuli in which a few sinusoidal vibrations with different frequencies are superimposed. We begin with an observation that such vibrotactile signals are analogous to musical chords where multiple notes are played simultaneously. A set of "vibrotactile chords" are designed based on the musical chords, and their degrees of consonance (harmony) that participants perceive are evaluated through a perception experiment. Experimental results indicate that the participants can robustly rate the degree of consonance of the vibrotactile chords and establish a well-defined relation of the degree of consonance to the base and chordal frequencies of a vibrotactile chord. These findings have direct implications to the design of complex vibrotactile signals that can be produced by current wideband actuators such as voice-coil, piezoelectric, and electroactive polymer actuators.

1 Introduction

In the past five years, vibration actuators have been significantly improved, especially due to the needs for mobile devices. Small and inexpensive commercial actuators using voice-coil, piezoelectric, and EAP (Electroactive Polymer) technologies are already available. These high-performance actuators have a wide frequency bandwidth, which can greatly diversify the vibrotactile stimuli we can create. However, our understandings on the perception of such complex vibrotactile signals are still far from complete in many aspects. In this paper, we consider one of the most fundamental cases, that is, two sinusoidal signals with different frequencies superimposed into one signal, and investigate their perceptual characteristics under the concept of *vibrotactile chord*.

In music, a chord refers to any set of notes that sound simultaneously. Individual notes in a chord are rather perceived as a whole. When they are perceived as harmonious, it is said that the degree of consonance is high for the chord. The degree of dissonance is the opposite concept. Analogously, each single-frequency vibrotactile signal in a multiple-frequency signal can be regarded as one note, and the mixed signal as a "vibrotactile chord." The central questions of the present study are whether we can robustly assess the degree of consonance from vibrotactile chords and if so, how the degree of consonance correlates to the frequency differences. This knowledge can contribute to

E.W. Cooper et al. (Eds.): HAID 2011, LNCS 6851, pp. 42–51, 2011.
© Springer-Verlag Berlin Heidelberg 2011

designing vibrotactile stimuli with diverse perceptual sensations and emotional impressions. For example, a signal with high consonance may be appropriate for a gentle reminder of appointments, while one with high dissonance can be useful for emergency alarms. In the rest of this paper, we present a set of vibrotactile chords designed based on musical chords and evaluate their degrees of consonance in order to find answers to the two research questions.

In Section 2, we briefly review related work and background. Section 3 describes the methods used in this study, and Section 4 reports experimental results. Discussion on the results is presented in Section 5, followed by conclusions in Section 6.

2   Related Work and Background

2.1   Related Work

Vibrotactile signals that include multiple frequency components can form various waveforms. Such superimposed signals may have a waveform envelope that varies considerably slower than the individual signals (see the left panel of Figure 1). In some cases, the property of one signal can be dominant over the others (right panel of Figure 1). The former delivers low-frequency pulse-like sensations, while the latter retains the smooth vibrational sensations of the original signals [10]. For these reasons, superimposed vibrotactile signals may feel disparate from single-frequency vibrations. For instance, Bensmaïa and Hollins compared the discriminability of two superimposed sinusoidal vibrations (10 + 30 Hz and 100 + 300 Hz) and demonstrated that their discriminabilities were very high with sensitivity indexes (d') as large as 3.0 [2].

In applications, amplitude-modulated vibrotactile signals are frequently used. They are a special case of signal superposition where two signals have the same amplitude. Examples that made use of amplitude modulation in haptics research includes tactile aids for the hearing impaired [4], tactile icons [3,14], and virtual texture rendering using vibrotactile stimuli only [1]. Recently, button-click sensations for virtual buttons displayed on a touchscreen were designed for a new dual-frequency actuator using signal superposition [9]. We expect that the recent advent of small, inexpensive, wideband actuators will further expand the use of complex vibrotactile stimuli in various applications.

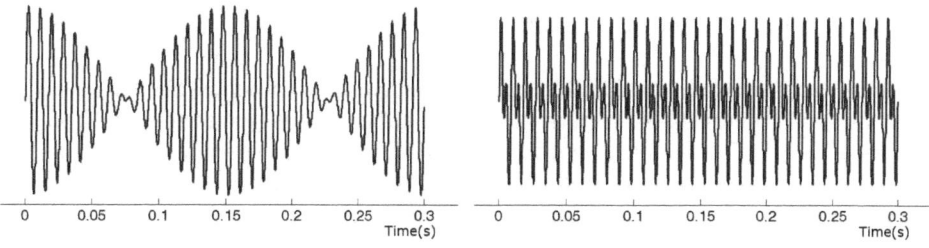

Fig. 1. Waveforms of two vibrotactile chords. (Left) 110 + 116.59 Hz. (Right) 110 + 220Hz. Both frequency components in each plot have the same amplitude.

2.2   Musical Chords and Their Perception

In western music, chords are commonly classed by their root note. For instance, the chord C Major can be described as a two-note (also called an interval) or a three-note chord of major quality built upon note C. An octave consists of 12 tones, so there are 12 different intervals in an octave. Each semitone is separated by one key on a piano, and the frequency ratio of two adjacent semitones is always $2^{\frac{1}{12}} : 1$ (about $1.059 : 1$) in a standard tuning. Therefore, the frequency of an octave-higher pitch is always twice high as the original pitch. The 12 intervals have their own names, determined by the number of semitones between their two tones, as listed in Table 1.

Table 1. Musical intervals (two-note chords)

Semitones	1	2	3	4	5	6
Name	Unison (1st)	minor 2nd	Major 2nd	minor 3rd	Major 3rd	Perfect 4th
Symbol	1	2m	2M	3m	3M	4
Semitones	7	8	9	10	11	12
Name	Augmented 4th	Perfect 5th	minor 6th	Major 6th	minor 7th	Major 7th
Symbol	4+	5	6m	6M	7m	7M

The perception of musical chords has been intensively studied since the late 19th century [15]. In particular, Helmholtz's theory pertaining to the consonance of musical chords seems to be relevant to the present study. H. von Helmholtz argued that consonance and dissonance in sound are determined by the level of acoustic beat[1] [5]. Two simultaneously played sound waves interfere with each other, and the human auditory system perceives them as a single combinational tone. In addition, if two pure tones are mixed, their frequency difference creates beats. In Helmholtz's theory, if the beats between the components are so intense that humans feel them as rough and unpleasant, the chords are regarded as dissonant tones. Otherwise they are regarded as consonant tones. He also explained that beats with frequencies near 33Hz are the most unpleasant to human auditory perception, while beats with frequencies less than 6 Hz or over 120 Hz are pleasant. This theory can account for the consonance perception of music to a large degree. However, it does not explain well the lower- or higher-frequency band where the frequency differences between semitones are too small or too large, respectively. Moreover, it is not applicable to instrumental tones, which include greatly richer harmonics.

In the early 20th century, C. F. Marmburg conducted an experiment about the smoothness of the 12 intervals of western music [8]. Table 2 summarizes the ranks of consonance according to Helmholtz's theory and Marmburg's experiment. These results indicate that the perceived smoothness is highly related to consonance in human auditory perception.

---

[1] A pulsation caused by the coincidence of the amplitudes of two oscillations of unequal frequencies, which has a frequency equal to the difference between the frequencies of the two oscillations (from dictionary.com).

Table 2. The ranks of consonance by Helmholtz's theory and Marmburg's experiment

Interval	Uni.	5P	4P	3M	4+	6M	6m	3m	7m	2M	7M	2m
Helmholtz	1	2	3	4	4	6	6	8	8	10	11	12
Marmburg	1	2	3	5	8	4	7	6	10	8	11	12

3   Methods

As stated earlier, the objectives of the present study are twofold:

Q1: Can we robustly evaluate the degree of consonance for vibrotactile chords?
Q2: How does the frequency difference in a vibrotactile chord affect the degree of consonance of the chord?

In this section, we present the methods used in a perceptual experiment carried out to answer these two research questions.

3.1   Participants

Sixteen native Korean university students enrolled in the author's institution (11 males and 5 females; 19 to 24 years old, average 21.7 years; 14 right-handed, 1 left-handed, and 1 ambidextrous) participated in this experiment. All participants reported that they had no difficulty in perceiving vibrations. Two participants had considerable experiences with haptic interfaces, while the others had little or no such experiences. All participants were paid for their help after the experiment.

3.2   Apparatus

A mini-shaker (Brüel & Kjær; model 4810) with a power amplifier (Brüel & Kjær; model 2718) produced all vibrotactile chords used in this experiment. The mini-shaker is a voice-coil actuator with a very wide frequency bandwidth (DC to 18 kHz) and high linearity. A mobile device mockup made of acrylic resin (Figure 2; $11.5 \times 4.5 \times 1.5$ cm, 91.7 g) was attached to the mini-shaker using a screw-type aluminum bracket. Participants grasped the mockup with their left hand to feel vibrations produced by the shaker. A triaxial accelerometer (Kistler; model 8765C) was attached to the mockup for closed-loop proportional control. A computer with a data acquisition board (National Instruments; model PCI-6251) controlled the shaker system at 10 kHz sampling rate. The linear relationships between input voltage amplitude and output vibration amplitude were calibrated for frequencies between 40 and 330 Hz at 10 Hz step, following the procedures detailed in [7]. Gains for in-between frequencies were linearly interpolated from the calibrated gains.

3.3   Stimuli

Each vibrotactile stimulus was two-second long and consisted of two frequency components. The base frequency was selected from 40, 55, 80 and 110 Hz. The chordal

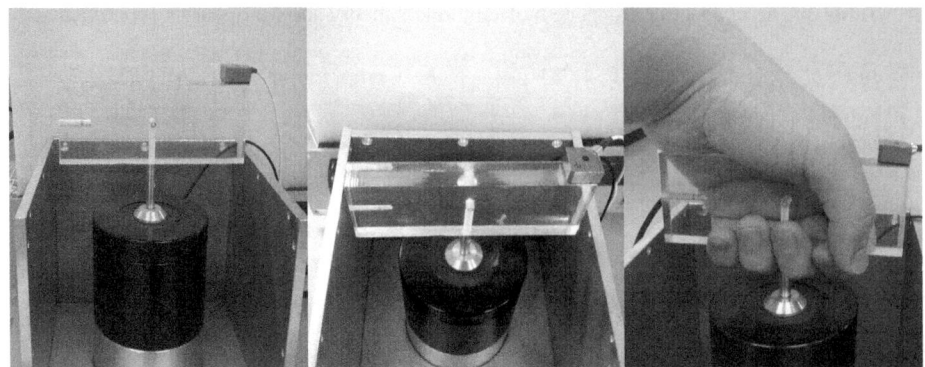

Fig. 2. Mini-shaker with a mobile device mockup. From left to right: front-view, top-view, and the participant's hand posture used in the experiment.

frequency was one of the 19 vibrotactile semitones with respect to the base frequency. For example, the chords for 110-Hz base frequency were the superimposed vibration pairs of 110 + 116.54 Hz, 110 + 123.47 Hz, 110 + 130.81 Hz, ···, 110 + 329.63 Hz. For comparison, the stimulus set also included single-frequency vibrations with only the base frequencies and doubled intensities. As a result, a total of 80 (4×20) stimuli were used in the experiment.

For each vibration signal, the amplitudes of its two frequency components were adjusted so that they resulted in the same perceived intensity. For this purpose, we used a psychophysical magnitude function similar to one given in [12]. Each frequency component had a perceived intensity of 10 according to the magnitude function. This intensity allowed clear perception of the superimposed signals. The magnitude function was recently measured while a vibration actuator was controlled under closed-loop control (that of [12] was measured under open-loop control). This new function shows higher perceived intensities for low-frequency (under 100 Hz) vibrations. Due to the limited space, we plan to report these data elsewhere.

3.4   Procedures

During the experiment, the participants were seated in front of a computer and grasped the mobile device mockup with their left hand in a comfortable posture. They wore the headphones that played pink noise to preclude any auditory cues. In each trial, a participant perceived a vibrotactile chord and answered its degree of consonance using a slider bar displayed on a monitor screen. The relative position of the slider bar was mapped to a number in 0–100. Two buttons were also shown on the screen to proceed to the next trial or repeat the previous trial, respectively.

The experiment consisted of nine sessions. The first session was for training and presented 20 vibrotactile chords evenly sampled from the 80 chords. The participants were instructed to establish criteria for assessing the degree of consonance of a vibrotactile chord during this session. The data of this session were not included in data analysis. Each of the next eight sessions presented 20 vibrotactile chords. As a result, each participant experienced the 80 vibrotactile chords twice, resulting in 160 consonance scores. The order of the chord presentation was randomized per participant. The participants were required to take a 5-minute rest between sessions to prevent fatigue and tactile adaptation.

All participants filled in pre- and post-experiment surveys. The pre-experiment survey was about the participants' demographic information such as their gender, handedness, and experience of haptic devices. In the post-experiment survey, the participants wrote down the criteria they used for consonance rating in a free form and the difficulty of establishing them on a 5-point Likert scale. In addition, the participants were provided with two sets of adjectives and asked to rate the agreement of each adjective to the perception of vibrotactile consonance and dissonance, respectively, on a 7-point Likert scale. The adjectives were extracted from [6] that included a set of adjectives suitable for vibration perception and experimenter-chosen adjectives commonly used to describe music perception. The adjective set for consonance was composed of those with positive meanings, while the set for dissonance was of those with negative meanings. The adjectives were given to the participants in Korean and their English translations are listed in Table 3.

3.5 Data Analysis

For each participant, we examined the correlation between the two repetitions of his/her consonance scores to confirm the participant could robustly assess the degree of consonance. If this inter-repetition correlation coefficient was below 0.5, we regarded the participant as incapable of robust assessment and excluded the data from further analysis. Then the degree of consonance of each vibrotactile chord was computed using the arithmetic mean across the rest of the participants.

4 Results

4.1 Inter-repetition Correlations

Only two participants resulted in consonance scores with their inter-repetition correlation coefficient less than 0.5. They also reported significant difficulties of establishing rating criteria in their post-experiment surveys. Their data were excluded from further analysis. The majority of the participants (14 out of 16) showed consistent scores of vibrotactile consonance. Their average inter-repetition correlation coefficient was 0.728 with a standard deviation of 0.135.

4.2 Degrees of Consonance

The average degrees of consonance of the 14 participants who passed the consistency test are shown in Figure 3 for the ratio of a chordal frequency to a base frequency. Important observations from the plot are: (1) For each base frequency, the base-frequency only signal shows a very high degree of consonance compared to the mixed signals. (2) Small frequency ratios (slightly over 1.0) result in the worst degrees of consonance,

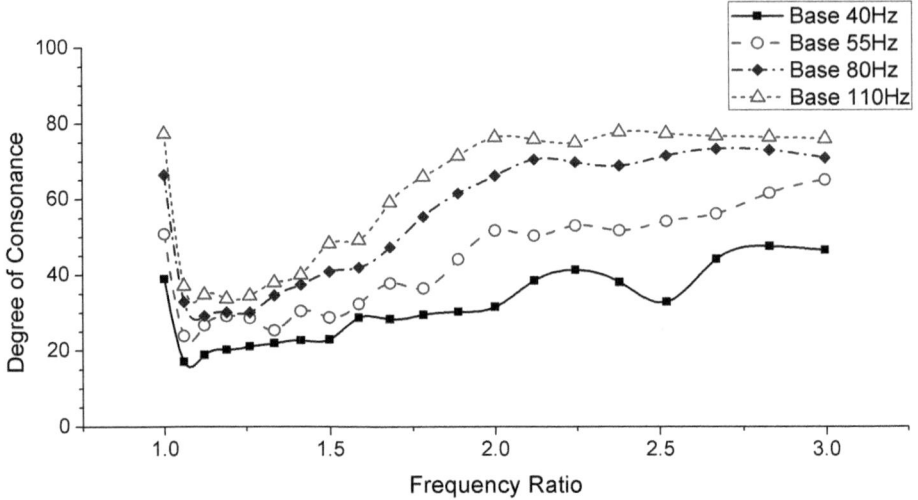

Fig. 3. Degree of consonance versus frequency ratio of a chordal frequency to a base frequency

as indicated by the abrupt drops in the plot. (3) Further increases in the frequency ratio improve the degree of consonance. (4) The degrees of consonance tend to become saturated when the frequency ratio is larger than about 2.0 for 80- and 110-Hz base frequencies. (5) The maximum degree of consonance for a base frequency is comparable to that of the base-frequency only for 80- and 110-Hz base frequencies, but it seems to be higher for 40- and 55-Hz base frequencies. (6) Higher base frequency improves the degree of consonance for the same frequency ratios.

4.3 Post-experiment Survey

The participants' responses to the difficulty of establishing criteria for vibrotactile consonance are shown in Figure 4. The average was 2.86 with a standard deviation of 0.74, where scores 1 and 5 represented "very difficult" and "very easy," respectively. This result suggests that the participants could assess the degrees of consonance of vibrotactile chords, but it appears to be slightly difficult.

In the free-form written questionnaire, participants frequently mentioned "smoothness," "comfortableness," "low intensity," and "continuity" as their consonance criteria. Those for dissonance were associated with "roughness," "irregularity," "high intensity," and "high fluctuation." In addition, the adjective rating results shown in Table 3 indicated that the sensations of "pleasant," "smooth," "even," "clear," and "clean" were highly relevant to consonance (scores higher than 5 in a 1–7 scale), whereas "jagged," "rough," "muddy," "bumpy," and "sparse" were to dissonance.

4.4 Summary of Results

Based on the experimental results reported above, the two research questions we raised earlier can now be answered.

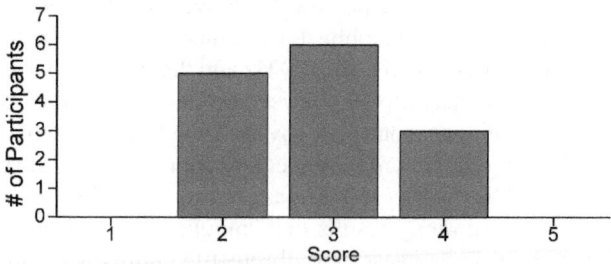

Fig. 4. Difficulty of establishing consonance criteria

Table 3. Adjective rating scores to vibrotactile consonance and dissonance (1–7 scale)

Consonance		Dissonance	
Adjective	Score	Adjective	Score
Pleasant	6.143	Jagged	6.643
Smooth	5.643	Rough	6.286
Even	5.571	Muddy	5.929
Clear	5.286	Bumpy	5.857
Clean	5.214	Sparse	5.786
Dense	4.929	Unpleasant	4.714
Gentle	4.642	Dark	2.929
Bright	3.214	Dirty	2.214
Beautiful	3.000	Blasphemous	2.000
Divine	2.071	Ugly	1.714

Q1: Can we robustly evaluate the degree of consonance for vibrotactile chords? 87.5% participants (14 out of 16) could evaluate the degree of consonance consistently. The degree of consonance showed a well-formulated relationship with the frequency ratio. The participants' subjectively-perceived difficulty of consonance evaluation was moderate (2.86 out of 5). Some adjectives were highly correlated with the degree of consonance, suggesting that the adjectives can be robust decision criteria. Therefore, the answer to Q1 is affirmative to a large extent.

Q2: How does the frequency difference in a vibrotactile chord affect its degree of consonance?

Figure 3 showed that the functional relationship between the degree of consonance and the frequency ratio of a chordal frequency to a base frequency is well defined. Detailed descriptions on the relation were given earlier in Section 4.2.

5 Discussion

Based on subjective descriptions, Tan classified sinusoidal vibrations into three groups along their frequency [13]. Vibrations in a 1–3 Hz band were described as a slow kinesthetic motion, those in 10–70 Hz as rough motion or fluttering, and those in 100–300 Hz as smooth vibration. In addition, we previously showed that the perceptual space of si-nusoidal vibrations perceived via a mobile device consists of two perceptual dimensions depending on their frequency, one for 40–100 Hz and the other for 100–250 Hz [6]. The results of the present study seem to be consistent with these earlier findings. Figure 3 showed that the degree of consonance improved as the base frequency increased from 40 Hz to 110 Hz. The ranges of chordal frequencies changed from 42.38–120 Hz (40 Hz base frequency) to 116.59-330 Hz (110 Hz base frequency). This result, along with the questionnaire and adjective rating results that smooth and pleasant stimuli were con-sidered as highly consonant, suggest that vibrotactile chords with smooth vibrational sensations are regarded as consonant. In contrast, low-frequency, fluttering, pulse-like, rough sensations seem to be the signs of dissonance.

Given a base frequency, the degree of consonance tended to monotonically increase with the chordal frequency (Figure 3). In particular, when the frequency ratio was slightly over 1.0, the degree of consonance showed the worst scores. The chordal fre-quencies in this range usually create clear low-frequency beats, which contribute to the fluttering, rough sensations. An example is given in the left panel of Figure 1. As the chordal frequency further increases, beats become to have higher frequency as shown in the right panel of Figure 1. This may explain the consonance improvements for the frequency ratio between 1.0 and 2.0. If the frequency ratios were over 2.0, two patterns were observed. For the two lower base frequencies (40 and 55 Hz), the degree of con-sonance was apt to further increase with the chordal frequency. These base frequencies produce very strong pulsating sensations. Their sensations might be being further neu-tralized by the chordal frequency components that impart smooth vibrational sensations. For the higher base frequencies (80 and 100 Hz) that are rather close to smooth vibra-tions, the degrees of consonance were saturated. This suggests that the sensations of the vibrotactile chords were already sufficiently smooth, and the use of higher chordal frequency did not affect the sensations further.

As the last remarks, the importance of beats in vibrotactile consonance perception appears to be analogous to Helmholtz's theory about musical consonance perception. In addition, the vibrotactile consonance plot shown in Figure 3 is very similar to those for the auditory degree of consonance [11]. These comparisons imply that understand-ing human consonance perception for vibrotactile chords may benefit from studying its similarity to auditory consonance perception theories. Research in this direction is currently on-going in our research group.

6   Conclusions

In this paper, we have proposed the concept of a vibrotactile chord and examined its validity as a means of studying the perceptual characteristics of complex vibrotac-tile stimuli. A perceptual experiment with 80 vibrotactile chords and 16 participants demonstrated that the majority of the participants could reliably assess the degree of consonance of vibrotactile chords. The experiment also unveiled a functional relation-ship between the frequency ratio of base and chordal frequencies and the degree of consonance. In addition, the subjective impressions associated with vibrotactile con-sonance and dissonance were also consistently described by the participants. Overall, the results bear some resemblance to auditory consonance perception, which will be our next research topic. The presented findings can be directly utilized for designing vibrotactile effects using recent wideband vibration actuators.

Acknowledgments. This work was supported in parts by an NRL program 2010-0018454 and a BRL program 2010-0019523 both from NRF and by an ITRC program NIPA-2011-C1090-1111-0008, all funded by the Korean government. We would like thank Dr. Hyesu Shin for her advices on the psychological theories of music.

References

1. Ahmaniemi, T., Marila, J., Lantz, V.: Design of dynamic vibrotactile textures. IEEE Transactions on Haptics 3(4), 245–256 (2010)
2. Bensmaïa, S., Hollins, M., Yau, J.: Vibrotactile intensity and frequency information in the Pacinian system: A psychophysical model. Perception & Psychophysics 67(5), 828–841 (2005)
3. Brown, L.M., Brewster, S.A., Purchase, H.C.: A first investigation into the effectiveness of tactons. In: Proceedings of the World Haptics Conference, pp. 167–176 (2005)
4. Goldstein Jr., M.H., Proctor, A.: Tactile aids for profoundly deaf children. The Journal of the Acoustical Society of America 77(1), 258–265 (1985)
5. von Helmholtz, H.: On the Sensations of Tone. Dover Publications, Inc., New York (1954)
6. Hwang, I., Choi, S.: Perceptual space and adjective rating of sinusoidal vibrations perceived via mobile device. In: Proceedings of the Haptics Symposium, pp. 1–8. IEEE, Los Alamitos (2010)
7. Israr, A., Choi, S., Tan, H.Z.: Detection threshold and mechanical impedance of the hand in a pen-hold posture. In: Proceedings of the IEEE/RSJ International Conference on Intelligent Robots and Systems (IROS), pp. 472–477 (2006)
8. Malmberg, C.F.: Perception of consonance and dissonance in music. Psychology Monograph 3(2), 93–133 (1918)
9. Park, G., Choi, S.: Tactile effect design and evaluation for virtual buttons on a mobile device touchscreen. To be presented in the 13th International Conference on Human-Computer Interaction with Mobile Devices and Services (MobileHCI). ACM, New York (2011)
10. Park, G., Choi, S.: Perceptual space of amplitude-modulated vibrotactile stimuli. To be presented in IEEE World Haptics Conference (2011)
11. Plomp, R., Levelt, W.J.M.: Tonal consonance and critical bandwidth. Journal of Acoustic Society of America 38, 548–560 (1965)
12. Ryu, J., Jung, J., Park, G., Choi, S.: Psychophysical model for vibrotactile rendering in mobile devices. Presence: Teleoperators and Virtual Environments 19(4), 1–24 (2010)
13. Tan, H.Z.: Information Transmission with a Multi-Finger Tactual Display. Ph.D. thesis, Massachusetts Institute of Technology (1996)
14. Ternes, D., MacLean, K.E.: Designing large sets of haptic icons with rhythm. In: Ferre, M. (ed.) EuroHaptics 2008. LNCS, vol. 5024, pp. 199–208. Springer, Heidelberg (2008)
15. Vickhoff, B.: A Perspective Theory of Music Perception and Emotion. Ph.D. thesis, University of Gothenburg (2008)

Vocal Manipulation Based on Pitch Transcription and Its Application to Interactive Entertainment for Karaoke

Kota Nakano[1], Masanori Morise[2], and Takanobu Nishiura[2]

[1] Graduate School of Science and Engineering, Ritsumeikan University,
1-1-1 Nojihigashi, Kusatsu, Shiga, 525-8577 Japan
[2] College of Information and Science, Ritsumeikan University,
1-1-1 Nojihigashi, Kusatsu, Shiga, 525-8577 Japan

Abstract. A real-time vocal manipulation system is described for improving karaoke. Karaoke is an interactive entertainment system where users sing along with recorded music, and it is used all over the world. However, although the users should sing with accurate pitch, it is difficult for the tone-deaf people to sing with accurate pitch. In this paper, a real-time vocal manipulation system is proposed to help tone-deaf people. The system consists of vocoder-based voice synthesis method that can synthesize the voiced sound with fundamental frequency (pitch) and spectral envelope (timbre). Vocal manipulation is achieved based on pitch transcription by replacing the pitch of a tone-deaf person with that of a professional singer. Subjective evaluation is carried out to verify the effectiveness of the proposed system. The results suggested that the proposed system can manipulate vocal sounds in real time.

Keywords: Vocal manipulation, Vocoder, Interactive entertainment, Karaoke.

1 Introduction

Karaoke is an interactive system where users sing along with recorded music, and it is used as engaging entertainment all over the world. Although many people have been using karaoke, tone-deaf users cannot enjoy the karaoke because of their singing ability. In karaoke, users should sing with the correct pitch for the song, whereas it is difficult for tone-deaf people to sing with the correct pitch. In other words, real-time pitch correction may help tone-deaf singers to enjoy singing, and it is expected that more interactive entertainment will be provided for tone-deaf singers.

Methods have been proposed to manipulate the pitch of a voice. Several commercial voice synthesizers that can manipulate pitch have been released [1,2]. In this paper, we focus on real-time pitch manipulation for karaoke and propose a system with pitch transcription for manipulating a singer's voice. The system generates the synthesized voice with the timbre of the user and the pitch of a professional singer in real time. The user can sing with the pitch of the professional singer.

E.W. Cooper et al. (Eds.): HAID 2011, LNCS 6851, pp. 52–60, 2011.
© Springer-Verlag Berlin Heidelberg 2011

The rest of this paper is organized as follows: Section 2 represents the overview of the vocal manipulation system based on pitch transcription. Section 3 discuss the implementation with the improved vocoder [3,4]. Section 4 represents and discusses the subjective evaluation to verify the effectiveness of the proposed system. Finally, Section 5 concludes this paper.

2   Voice Manipulation Based on Pitch Transcription

Morphing-based singing design has already been proposed [5,6,7,8,9], and the effectiveness of the pitch correction has been suggested by conventional studies. Vocal manipulation based on pitch transcription is one of the approaches to help the tone-deaf people in karaoke.

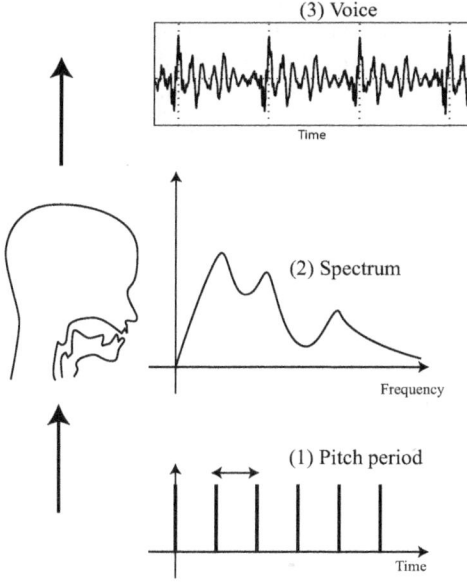

Fig. 1. Voiced sound and its generation process

Figure. 1 illustrates a voice generation process. Voiced sound is a periodic signal. The voiced sound can be defined as a combination of a excitation signal and a spectral envelope. The combination can be written as the next formula.

$$S(\omega) = H(\omega)G(\omega) \tag{1}$$

$S(\omega)$ is a spectrum of voiced sound, $H(\omega)$ is spectral envelope and $G(\omega)$ is a spectrum of excitation signal. The excitation signal $G(\omega)$, in our voiced sound, is a periodic signal and can define a fundamental frequency. The fundamental frequency is the inverse of its period, which may be defined as the smallest member of the infinite set of time shift that leave a signal invariant. The subjective pitch of a sound usually depends on its fundamental frequency. In addition, each period has a similar impulse response. The spectral envelope $H(\omega)$ is harmonic information on the frequency domain. The spectral envelope corresponds to timbre, and it determines voice personality and phoneme in voiced sound. The fundamental frequency depends on vocal chord vibration and the spectral envelope depends on vocal tract in voiced sound, and they are independent each other. It is expected that the pitch transcription will be achieved by analysis and synthesis based on separating the voice into a fundamental frequency and a spectral envelope.

2.1   Framework of the Proposed System

The proposed system is based on pitch transcription by replacing the pitch contour of the user with that of a professional singer.

Figure 2 illustrates the flowchart of the proposed system. The voice of a professional singer is analyzed, and his or her pitch is stored for transcription in preliminary processing. In real-time processing, the voice of the user is analyzed, and the system synthesizes the output with the timbre of the user and the pitch of the professional singer. The processing can be seen in the following formulas.

$$S_p(\omega) = H_p(\omega)G_p(\omega), \tag{2}$$
$$S_u(\omega) = H_u(\omega)G_u(\omega). \tag{3}$$

$S_p(\omega)$ and $S_u(\omega)$ are spectra of sounds voiced by a professional singer and a user. $H_p(\omega)$ and $H_u(\omega)$ are timbres of their sounds. $G_p(\omega)$ and $G_u(\omega)$ are spectra of the excitation signal of their sounds. Accordingly, the manipulated sound $S_m(\omega)$ by pitch transcription can be also seen in the following formula.

$$S_m(\omega) = H_u(\omega)G_p(\omega). \tag{4}$$

The manipulated sound is synthesized from the pitch contour of a professional singer and the timbre of a user.

Vocoder has been used to manipulate voiced sound. The proposed system employes a vocoder-based method for pitch manipulation.

2.2   Vocoder-Based Core Technology for the Framework

The original vocoder [3] analyzes voice in terms of a fundamental frequency (pitch), a spectral envelope (timbre), and synthesizes a voiced sound from these parameters. Although the vocoder tries to independently manipulate fundamental frequency and spectral envelope in a human voice, the quality of the synthesized sound is still poor. Various improved vocoders such as the cepstral vocoder [10] and LPC vocoder [11] have been proposed for high-quality synthesis. TANDEM-STRAIGHT [12], which is an improved vocoder, can synthesize the voice that sounds as natural as the input voice, and manipulate the pitch

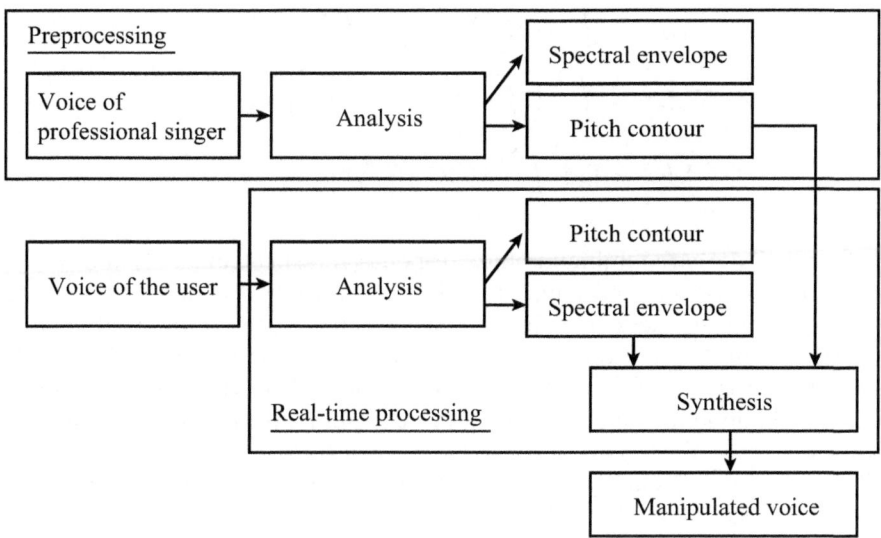

Fig. 2. The system flow of vocal-assistant system

and timbre without deterioration. TANDEM-STRAIGHT meets the requirements that the synthesized voice is high quality enough to sound completely natural. On the other hand, the voice manipulation process, in the proposed system, has to process the data in real time for karaoke. TANDEM-STRAIGHT is nevertheless incapable of real-time processing because it would require too much computational power. We tried to simplify and reduce the required computational power in TANDEM-STRIAGHT for real-time manipulation.

3   Simplified High-Quality Vocoder

TANDEM-STRAIGHT requires 854 % of the input sound's time length for analysis and synthesis although it can synthesize high quality sound. In other words, 1 second of input sound would require 8.54 seconds of processing time. This is far too long for real-time voice synthesis to be used in karaoke. The TANDEM-STRAIGHT algorithm analyzes voiced sound and estimates not only the fundamental frequency and the spectral envelope but also aperiodic ratio as a third parameter. Our voiced sound has aperiodic fluctuation, and the aperiodic ratio corresponds to it. The aperiodic ratio estimation is the bottle neck of its analysis and synthesis. We employed a method for aperiodic signal extraction in voice instead of aperiodic ratio estimation to simplify TANDEM-STRAIGHT [4]. In our method, the excitation signal in voiced sound is obtained with convoluting inverse filter of the spectral envelope based on a minimum phase response. The minimum phase response can be obtained by a Hilbert transform of the logarithmic spectrum. The Hilbert transform can be calculated with the following formulas.

$$x_m(t) = \int_{-\infty}^{\infty} \exp\left(X_m(\omega)\right) e^{2\pi j\omega t} d\omega, \tag{5}$$

$$X_m(\omega) = \int_{0}^{\infty} \left(\int_{-\infty}^{\infty} X(\omega) e^{2\pi j\omega t} d\omega \right) e^{-2\pi j\omega t} dt, \tag{6}$$

$$X(\omega) = \log \left| \int_{-\infty}^{\infty} x(t) e^{-2\pi j\omega t} dt \right|. \tag{7}$$

$x_m(t)$ and $X_m(\omega)$ are minimum phase response and spectrum. $x(t)$ and $X(\omega)$ are observed response and spectrum. The Hilbert transform is related to a notion of casuality or one-sidedness. The first transform is integrated from negative infinite to positive infinite on frequency domain, and the second transform is integrated from 0 to positive infinite on time domain. The Hilbert transform is applied to the logarithmic amplitude spectrum, and the minimum phase spectrum can be obtained.

The obtained signal is a combination of a periodic signal and an aperiodic signal. The aperiodic signal is extracted by reducing the power of the pulse which corresponds to the periodic signal. The extracted aperiodic signal is used for synthesis to bypass the aperiodic ratio estimation for real-time processing. Accordingly, the simplified high-quality vocoder has been able to reduce 96 % of the processing time [4]. The simplified vocoder can process the data in real time, and it is employed in the proposed voice manipulation system.

3.1 Synchronization of Pitch Contours

The proposed system requires that the pitch contour of the user is synchronized with that of a professional singer because it is impossible for real-time processing to compensate the time differences with current technology. In other words, the user should sing along with the voice of the professional singer, which is also a requirement for karaoke. It is therefore expected that their pitch contours are temporally synchronized. In this paper, we first confirm whether two pitch contours sung by two singers are temporally synchronized.

We recorded the voices sung along with recorded music, and subjects were a amateur singer and a professional singer. Pitch contour was estimated with TANDEM-STRAIGHT as an accurate pitch estimation method. Figure 3 represents the pitch contours of two singers. The horizontal axis represents time, and the vertical axis represents pitch (fundamental frequency; F0). Source F0 represents the pitch contour of the amateur singer, and target F0 represents that of the professional singer.

In Fig. 3, we could confirm that pitch contours were temporally synchronized. Therefore, we may be able to manipulate vocal sounds without time alignment. By using the proposed system, the user can sing with the pitch of the professional singer.

However, since the voice section of two pitch contours are slightly different, sound quality of the synthesized vocal may decrease.

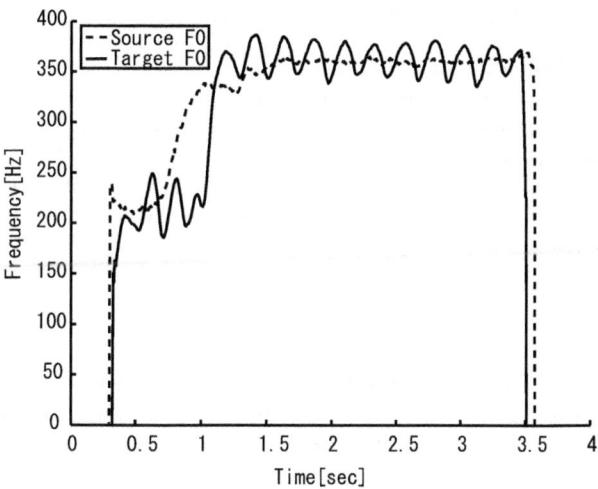

Fig. 3. Pitch contours of two singers

4   Evaluation

Subjective evaluation was carried out to demonstrate the effectiveness of the proposed system. In this paper, satisfaction rating of the proposed system was evaluated.

Table 1 shows the experimental conditions of the evaluation. The employed songs for the system is two Japanese songs, Anokanewo Narasunowa Anata and Kawa no Nagare no You-ni. A female semi-professional singer's voice was used. 10 subjects (8 males and 2 females) participated in the evaluation.

Table 1. The experimental conditions

Category	Specification
Computer	MacOSX (CPU: Core2Duo 2.4 GHz, Memory: 8 GB)
Audio interface	TAPCO LINK.FireWire 4x6
Microphone	AKG C214
Loudspeaker	BOSE Micro Music Monitor
Sampling rate	44.1 kHz
Audio bit depth	32 bit
Background noise	31 dBA

Subjects evaluated the proposed system using the 6 choices shown in Tab 2. Excellent, Good and Fairly good represent the positive answers for the proposed system, whereas Poor, Bad and Fairly bad represent the negative answers for the proposed system.

Table 2. The choices for the evaluation

Choices	Evaluation of the system
Excellent	Proposed system is much superior to the conventional karaoke
Good	Proposed system is superior to the conventional karaoke
Fairly good	Both are fairly good
Poor	Proposed system is inferior to the conventional karaoke
Bad	Proposed system is much inferior to the conventional karaoke
Fairly poor	Both are fairly poor

4.1 Results

Figure 4 represents the experimental result. 50 % of subjects indicated that the proposed system was superior to the conventional karaoke, and 70 % of subjects positively indicated the proposed system. However, 30 % of subjects indicated that the proposed system was inferior to conventional karaoke because of the lower sound quality of the synthesized voice.

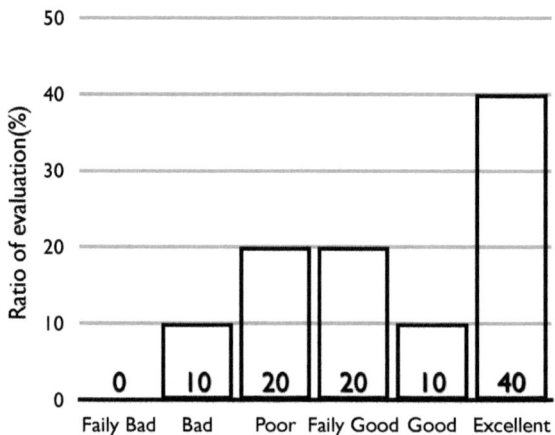

Fig. 4. Result of system evaluation

4.2 Discussion

As a result, 70 % of the subjects indicated that the proposed system was effective to help users in karaoke. On the other hand, 30 % of subjects indicated that the proposed system was inferior to the conventional karaoke. Since this system is for the tone-deaf people, it is not necessary for people that have good singing ability to use the proposed system. In the next evaluation, users with normal singing ability should be excepted from the subjects.

Since the sound quality of the synthesized voice was inferior to the original voice, several subjects may have negatively evaluated the proposed system. Improvement of the sound quality is one of the important future efforts. Latency is not major issue in this experiment because the songs for evaluation were slow-tempo music. An evaluation with high-tempo music should be carried out in the future work. Furthermore, visual interaction generally used for conventional karaoke will be implemented in the next release of the proposed system.

5 Conclusion

Vocal manipulation method based on pitch transcription was proposed to help tone-deaf people to sing similar to the professional singer. Pitch transcription for vocal manipulation was achieved by synthesis based on the timbre of the user and the pitch of the professional singer. The system can synthesize natural vocal with the timbre of the user in real time. The key point is that we extract aperiodic signal from the input voiced sound instead of relying on real-time processing which would require too much computational power.

The subjective evaluation was carried out to verify the effectiveness of the proposed system. Although the synthesized vocal was inferior to the original vocal in sound quality. The results indicated that the vocal manipulation was effective to sing with the appropriate pitch. This result suggested that the proposed system based on pitch transcription was effective to help tone-deaf people.

Improvement of the voice synthesis method is one of the important issues for future work. Future work will also include research on implementing the visual interaction generally used for conventional karaoke.

Acknowledgments. This research was partly supported by Ono Acoustics Research Fund and Grants-in-Aid for Scientific Research funded by MEXT Japan.

References

1. Kenmochi, H., Ohshita, H.: VOCALOID - commercial singing synthesizer based on sample concatenation. In: Proc. Interspeech 2007, pp. 4009–4010 (2007)
2. Hidebrand, H.A.: Pitch detection and intonation correction apparatus and method. U.S. Patent 5,973252 (1999)
3. Dudley, H.: Remaking speech. J. Acoust. Soc. Am. 11(2), 169–177 (1939)
4. Nakano, K., Morise, M., Nishiura, T.: Proposal of a new vocoder for real-time synthesis of speech signal with high quality. In: Proc. ICA 2010, PaperID:332 (2010)
5. Cano, P., Loscos, A., Bonada, J., de Boer, M., Serra, X.: Voice morphing system for impersonating in karaoke applications. In: Proc. ICMC, pp.109–112 (2000)
6. Morise, M., Onishi, M., Kawahara, H., Katayose, H.: v.morish 2009: A morphing-based singing design interface for vocal melodies. In: Natkin, S., Dupire, J. (eds.) ICEC 2009. LNCS, vol. 5709, pp. 185–190. Springer, Heidelberg (2009)
7. Kawahara, H., Nisimura, R., Irino, T., Morise, M., Takahashi, T., Banno, H.: Temporally variable multi-aspect auditory morphing enabling extrapolation without objective and perceptual breakdown. In: Proc. ICASSP 2009, pp. 3905–3908 (2009)
8. Kawahara, H., Nishikara, R., Irino, T., Morise, M., Takahashi, T., Banno, H.: Higi-quality and light-weight voice transformation enabling extrapolation without perceptual and objective breakdown. In: Proc. ICASSP 2010, pp. 4818–4821 (2010)

9. Uchimura, Y., Banno, H., Itakura, F., Kawahara, H.: Study of manipulation method of voice quality based on the vocal tract area function. In: Proc. Interspeech 2008, pp.1084–1087 (2008)
10. Oppenheim, A.V.: A speech analysis-synthesis system based on homomorphic filtering. J. Acoust. Soc. Am. 45(2), 458–465 (1969)
11. Atal, B.S., Hanauer, M.R.: Speech Analysis and Synthesis by Linear Predictive of the Speech Wave. J. Acoust. Soc. Am. 50(2), 637–655 (1971)
12. Kawahara, H., Morise, M., Banno, H., Takahashi, T., Irino, T.: TANDEM-STRAIGHT: A temporally stable power spectral representation for periodic signals and applications to interference-free spectrum, f0, and aperiodicity estimation. In: Proc. ICASSP 2008, pp. 3933–3936 (2008)

Calm Down – Exploiting Sensorimotor Entrainment in Breathing Regulation Application

Antti Pirhonen and Kai Tuuri

Department of Computer Science and Information Systems,
PO Box 35, FI-40014 University of Jyväskylä, Finland
{antti.pirhonen,kai.tuuri}@jyu.fi

Abstract. Various phenomena in human life are related to different kinds of rhythms. Not only are our bodily functions based on rhythms, but also much of the interaction with our environment is related to them. In this study, we explore breathing regulation and how it could be supported with an interactive application. The application is based on the concept of entrainment, in which two interacting entities adjust to a common rhythm. The focus is in the design of interaction elements which support entrainment process. A user study of a prototype application is also reported in the paper. The results indicate that the approach is promising and has potential in opening new perspectives to human-computer interaction.

Keywords: breathing regulation, entrainment, multimodal interaction.

1 Introduction

The human being is tied up to many kinds of rhythms. Most of them are connected to each other. We can effortlessly observe several physical rhythms in our body, for instance breathing and heart rate. They reflect the different qualities of the states of the human being in the environment, feelings such as relaxation, stress and physical effort. However, not only do these rhythms reflect reactions, but also vice versa, by affecting them the state of a human being can be changed [1]. For example, slow breathing may express a high level of relaxation, but also by consciously slowing down breathing frequency it is possible to reach higher levels of relaxation. This, in turn, can be observed in the slower heart beat rate.

Synchronisation to external rhythm is a common and well documented phenomenon of human behaviour [2, 3], which is demonstrated even among infants [4]. In our everyday experience, we may notice that listening to music while walking tends to change the walking rhythm towards that of the music. Such rhythmic engagement is a unidirectional process: the music is received and the listener adapts to the rhythm. If these two, the music and the listener, are in reciprocal relation with each other, we have to expand the view from mere synchronisation.

In disciplines such as physiology, psychology, neurorehabilitation and music therapy, the process in which two entities interactively assume a common rhythm, is usually called *entrainment* [2, 5]. We use entrainment as a central concept in this

E.W. Cooper et al. (Eds.): HAID 2011, LNCS 6851, pp. 61–70, 2011.
© Springer-Verlag Berlin Heidelberg 2011

study to refer to the process in which relaxation is pursued through interaction with a breathing regulation application.

In this paper, we present a case study in which bodily engagement has a particularly important role. The case study is about an application, in which relaxation is sought after by controlling breathing rhythm. The proposed concept is based on an idea of "movement" in which one's breathing would be conformed naturally and effortlessly, either consciously or subconsciously. Movement would thus illustrate breathing oscillation patterns in real-time. Basically, the application would utilise the method of *breathing entrainment intervention*, which has been successfully used in clinical music therapy [1]. After presenting the application, focusing on the design principles and design process, we will report the central findings of a concise user study.

2   Breath Rate Application: The Making of

2.1   Background

Breathing is one of our vital autonomous functions. It is a part of our autonomous system and takes care of the necessary delivery of oxygen. However, even though it is involuntarily controlled, we are also able to control it consciously. This ability has been found useful for several purposes, since the breathing rate has an impact on a number of psycho-physiological phenomena. In other words, while autonomous breathing control is based on a variety of needs of the body, by controlling breathing rhythm other functions of the body can be affected. Being in constant reciprocal connections to the whole body, breathing is a prominent function to be utilised when aiming at controlling the physical and mental phenomena.

Slow and deep breathing (so-called *paced breathing*) has been found beneficial in the treatment of e.g. stress, anxiety, insomnia, panic disorder and many other health and well-being-related conditions [6, 7]. Applications which help in the strive towards paced breathing, widely referred to as device guided breathing (DGB [7]), are interactive in nature; they monitor the actual breathing while giving support in reaching the recommended rate and breathing form (usually prolonged exhale).

In this study, we do not aim at a full DGB application in that we do not intend to include any monitoring of actual breathing in it. Our objective is to study how breathing control could be supported with a multimodal application. In practice, this implies the idea of animation and sound illustrating the breathing rate. Although similar implementations have been used in more entertainment-orientated products (such as Wii Fit [8]), the focus of our interest is in how users of these kinds of applications would experience the synchronisation to the suggested breathing frequency.

2.2   Design Task and General Principles

Our task was to design and evaluate a prototype application for breathing regulation. The initial idea was to present audio-visual movement back and forth, schematically referring to the periodic structure of breath oscillation. The research task was to explore the process in which the user synchronises her breathing to the oscillation of the application. The setting is rather analogous with the relationship between a conductor of an orchestra and the musicians who follow the gestures of the conductor.

The design is based on an innate human capability of imitation [2,9]. Imitation is a fundamental way for human beings to adapt to the environment. As already stated, a central concept is entrainment, which implies the synchronisation to an external rhythm by *embodied attunement* [2].

The underlying sensorimotor mechanisms create a close link between perceived movement and bodily experience; they effortlessly allow us to understand the movement as "mirrored", i.e., they reflect one's own motor activity. Such *motoric* element involved in perception has been found to integrate multiple modalities [10] and ultimately convert simple external physical event to a highly embodied experience [2, 9].

The prototype aims at combining animation and audio to a coherent whole, in which both modalities support each other by referring to the mutual movement patterns. On the other hand, the essential information is redundantly in audio and visual format, thus enabling individual preferences and cognitive styles to be exploited [11]. This is achieved by a design strategy in which the same *design concepts* are expressed in the user interface in both presentation modalities.

Design Concepts

The applied design concepts refer to schematic movement patterns, analogous to image schemas [12]. The underlying assumption was that these patterns are associated with the kinaesthesia of breathing:

- Expanding…shrinking – relates e.g. to the chest movements
- Ascending…descending – in the breathing cycle, the overall rise of tension and then release
- Filling…emptying – air flow to and from the body
- High…low flow rate – current and pressure of air
- Approaching…receding – metaphorical expression of proximity: approaching in inhale, receding in exhale

These, highly overlapping and intertwined design concepts were intended to be captured in embodied imitative processes. These, in turn, would facilitate the entrainment of breathing patterns.

Breathing rhythm or the turning points from inhale to exhale would of course be able to indicate with very simple signs. However, since breathing is a dynamic and continual process, we found a concept which stresses these qualities more appropriate than indication of turning points only. The application should therefore continuously indicate the phase of breathing cycle (breath in onset and a slope … inhale apex … breathe out onset and slope … exhale apex …), the amplitude of the oscillation and the speed of movement.

Interaction Model

Entrainment is an interactive process between two agents, in this case the user and the application. Ideally, the setting to be unquestionably interactive, both the user and the system should have impact on each other. In such a system, the application would take into account the actual breathing rate and phase. This information could then be utilised in gradually inducing the user towards the recommended kind of breathing. That is to say, the application could first imitate the breathing of the user, but then carefully slow down to the intended oscillation form and rate.

In the current version of the application, no sensors for monitoring breathing were used, so it can be argued that our implementation is only partial. However, we argue that there is still a kind of interaction in the user's mind, analogous to the entrainment (or synchronisation) with playback of recorded music. When the user receives music, or in our case multimodal stimulus, the mind of the user it is in an intensive interaction with the breathing regulation and other organic systems.

Technically speaking, the application has some interactive elements as well, since the oscillation rate could be adjusted to agree with the user's preference of a relaxed rate of breathing. In addition, the user could choose between two alternative oscillation waveforms.

Prototype UI-Elements

Visual
The central visual object in the application is a circular animated shape (Figure 1), which is expanding (inhale) and shrinking (exhale). In accordance with the oscillation pattern, this indicator circle element also

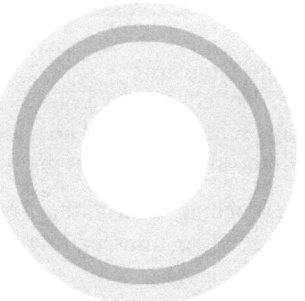

- changes its opacity between 0% and 100%
- changes its colour saturation between grey and vivid blue.

Change in the shape size refers to expanding/ascending…shrinking/descending scheme (corresponds to chest movements). Changes in the opacity and saturation refer to approaching/appearing …receding/dissolving scheme (the shape comes close and then

Fig. 1. Screen shot of the animation

withdraws). The change in saturation also refers to filling…emptying scheme; colour saturation of the shape corresponds to the amount of air in the lungs.

The amplitude of oscillation, i.e., the boundaries of expanding-shrinking movement are also visualised with an area of solid background colour (Figure 1). The apices of the oscillation (minimum and maximum points) are indicated visually with smooth "beat" effects. At the minimum value, the inner circle inside the boundary area makes a pulsation comprising a sharp change of colour followed with a gradual change back to white (in 600 ms duration). At the maximum value the effect is based on similar colour pulse, but it occurs as an "echo" circle outside the boundary circle (expanding beyond boundaries as it dissolves). These effects denote the inhale and exhale onsets, respectively.

Audio
The presentation consists of three separate sound elements. Two of them are based on filtered noise; the third one is based on a filtered musical tone.

- Noise element 1 (in the lower spectrum):

  — Source: pre-processed white noise. Very low frequencies, that sound like rumble, are filtered out. This source loops on playback.
  — Low-pass filter is applied to the source. The cut-off frequency dynamically travels between predetermined minimum (e.g., 126 Hz) and maximum (e.g., 316 Hz) frequency values in accordance with the oscillation.
  — This element results in a pattern which resembles waves in the seaside. The effect reflects the schemes of expanding…shrinking (the noise bandwidth) ascending…descending (corresponds to, e.g., rising level of tension in inhale and tension release in exhale) and approaching…receding (metaphor of, e.g., approaching and receding water's edge in a beach).

- Noise element 2 (in the higher spectrum):

  — Uses the same noise source as the element 1.
  — A narrow band-pass filter is applied to the source. The filter band dynamically travels between predetermined minimum (e.g., 1000 Hz) and maximum (e.g., 1778 Hz) frequency values in accordance with the oscillation pattern. The bandwidth of the filter is also slightly adjusted: it expands during breath in slope and narrows during breath out slope.
  — The volume of this element is also (mapped – synchronised?) to the speed of oscillation movement. This results in higher volumes for faster movements and softer volume for slower movements. This effect is intended to correspond to the amount of air flow in breathing (high flow-rate => high volume).
  — This element complements the effect of noise element 1, resembling either wind noise or waves in the seaside. The effect of element 2 especially refers to the scheme of ascending…descending (corresponds to, e.g., rising level of muscle tension in inhale and tension release in exhale) and the scheme of flow rate (corresponds to air flow of either wind or breathing).

- Musical tone

  — A sample of didgeridoo recording as a source. The source loops on playback (as a continuous drone-sound).
  — The element is designed as an optional addition which would facilitate the meditative and relaxing function of the sound.
  — The volume of the element follows the oscillation pattern; complementing the rising intensity and tension towards the maximum point of oscillation.
  — The spectrum of the tone is also dynamically varied by two filters:

    1. Resonant filter: a narrow-band 14 dB boost filter with a moving center frequency in accordance with the oscillation function (e.g., between 224-794 Hz). The travelling filter band results in ascending and descending "melody" due to the boosted harmonics of the didgeridoo tone.
    2. Low-pass filter with a moving cut-off frequency (at an octave above the resonant centre). The frequency spectrum of the tone expands during inhale and shrinks during exhale.

Interactive Controls of the Prototype

Even if the basic idea of the prototype looks and sounds really simple, there are a number of parameters whose ideal value is impossible to know without user studies. Therefore, we included in the prototype ten interactive control elements, with which a user would be able to tailor the application. These were

- Oscillation frequency: 4..15 (1/100 Hz)
- Default/Alternative waveform type (oscillation pattern)
- Master volume 0..7
- Noise element switch: On/Off

    − Amplitude of noise pattern 1..9
    − Brightness of the noise 1..9

- Drone element switch: On/Off (refers to the didgeridoo-tone described above)
- Animation: On/Off

    − Amplitude of the animation 1..9
    − Indication of apices (inhale->exhale, exhale->inhale): On/Off

These controls were included in the prototype that was used in the evaluation for two purposes. First, we could see diversity among user preferences. This information is be useful when deciding which parameters should be customisable. That is, if there is not much variation concerning a certain parameter, the mean of the choices would probably work nicely as a fixed value. That value is the second thing to be found in the evaluation. However, if there is a lot of variation in the chosen values of a certain parameter, it might be wise to keep that parameter customisable in the future version.

2.3 Evaluation

A concise evaluation of the application was carried out with 6 participants (M=4, F=2). All the participants were research and teaching staff at the faculty of Information Technology in the University of Jyväskylä, Finland.

Each participant tried the application individually, without prior instructions. Only in the beginning of the session, the participant learned what they need to do . The introduction (read aloud by the researcher) was as follows:

"We are testing an application, which is supposed to help in relaxation. The means to relaxation is slowing down breathing rate. On the screen you can see an animation which illustrates the desired breathing pattern. Watch and listen, relax, and gradually try to conform to the animation. First adjust the volume and breathing rate to a comfortable level from here [researcher points the controller on the screen]. *You can also try an alternative breathing pattern from here* [researcher points the controller on the screen]." In addition, the participants were encouraged to think aloud.

After approximately 3 minutes trial period, new instruction was given:

"You are now able to adjust some of the properties of the animation. Try to tailor it so as to make it suitable for even a lengthy relaxation session, and that it supports your relaxation as well as possible. First try the effect of each option."

The participant then did what was asked of them, thinking aloud (the amount of thinking aloud varied a lot, though). This phase took approximately 5 minutes, after which the researcher saved the settings in a database. The choices made by the participants, when they tailored the application, are summarised in Table 1.

Table 1. Choices among options

Option / Part. #	Oscillation frequency	Waveform type	Master volume	Noise elements	Drone element	Variation width	Volume level	Animation switch	Beat markers	Variation width
1	9	0	1	1	0	3	5	1	1	5
2	8	0	1	1	0	6	5	1	1	6
3	9	0	1	1	0	1	2	1	0	2
4	15	0	1	1	0	9	1	1	0	3
5	8	1	6	1	0	3	9	1	0	7
6	9	0	1	1	1	2	2	1	0	2
Mean	9,67	0,17	1,83	1,00	0,17	4,00	4,00	1,00	0,33	4,17
SD	2,66	0,41	2,04	0,00	0,41	2,97	2,97	0,00	0,52	2,14

Table 1 shows all the choices made by the participants:

- *Oscillation frequency*. The participants were advised to adjust the frequency to a comfortable level, but this was only for the needs of this study; in the future versions, the application should be interactive in that it can be dynamically adjusted on the basis of target frequency and the actual breathing rate.
- *Waveform type*. All but one participant changed the default waveform. On the basis of the think-aloud data, this is partly due to the fact that the difference between the two was not quite evident to the participant.
- *Master volume*: 5 out of 6 participants adjusted the volume as low as possible (1 in scale 0..7). This evokes a question, would they have adjusted it even lower if it would have been possible? None of the participants mentioned anything like that, however. Since the actual volume depends on the adjustment of the application, the adjustment of the computer sound and the adjustment of amplifier, the conclusion concerning the volume is that sound is important but it should not be loud. If the adjustment property will be included in the forthcoming versions, the scale should be changed to enable fine-adjustment in low volume levels.
- *Noise elements*: Chosen by all. Conclusion: Probably no need to be disabled.
- *Drone element*: Only one participant checked the option. The value of the drone sound probably is a matter of preference. It is interesting that the same participant who preferred the drone also preferred the sound feedback over the visual elements (see below). Conclusion: Could be kept as an optional and adjustable property.
- *Variation width* (of the sound): Values from minimum to maximum were quite evenly chosen. However, in the discussions, this property did not appear very

important to the participants. Conclusion: Could be kept as an adjustable property.

- *Volume level* (brightness): Evenly distributed choices between the extremes. Conclusion: to be kept adjustable.
- *Animation* (on/off): All participants wanted to have this, no need for the ability to switch it off.
- *Beat markers* (in animation): Only two participants chose to have this visual sign. Probably not necessary or might need redesign.
- *Variation width* (of the animation): Evenly distributed choices between 2 and 7 (in scale 1..9). Should be kept as such.

Finally, the participants were asked to fill in a short questionnaire. It was a tailored version of NASA Task Load Index (TLX) [13]. In it, each participant was asked to evaluate 7 issues: Understandability (bad-good), mental load caused by the following of animation and sound (low-high), the most beneficial element in finding the right breathing pattern (sound-animation), own performance (bad-good), frustration (low-high), pleasantness (low-high), calming effect (low-high). Each of these issues was evaluated in 21-point scale, in which the participant was asked to tick off the perceived level. The results are in Table 2. The scale has been converted to number scale 0..10.

The figures of Table 2 are very motivating for further development of the application. As one can see, the application was perceived as highly understandable, pleasant and having a strong calming effect. Mental load was found fairly low, frustration very low. Five participants found animation more essential than sound. However, it is important to remember that in some situations, interaction with an application might become more reliant on sounds. As omnidirectionally radiating elements, sounds are not dependent on gaze. The participants ranked their own performance high, which probably indicates high motivation and positive attitude towards the task and the concept.

Table 2. Results of a subjective evaluation

Property / Part. #	Understand ability	Mental load	Sound vs. animation	Own performance	Frustration	Pleasantness	Calming effect
1	8,5	1,5	7,5	9	0,5	9	9
2	7	6,5	9,5	6	4,5	8	7,5
3	7,5	0,5	8,5	6,5	0,5	5	6
4	8	3,5	7	5	0,5	8,5	7
5	8,5	3,5	7	6	1,5	6,5	6,5
6	7	5	1,5	6,5	1,5	7,5	7,5
Mean	7,75	3,42	6,83	6,50	1,50	7,42	7,25
SD	0,69	2,20	2,79	1,34	1,55	1,46	1,04

3   Conclusions and Discussion

The reported case study included the first step in the creation of an interactive relaxation application. The prototype did not have all the functionality and interactivity that could be implemented. The foremost restriction was that we did not use any sensors to monitor the actual breathing of the participants. As discussed above, that kind of technology would enable dynamic adjustment of the frequency and possibly oscillation pattern. However, we argue that the issues we were able to discover with the current prototype are the most important when making assessments about the applicability of the concept that is based on sensorimotor entrainment.

Experimental results demonstrated that the concept is a promising basis for the development of relaxation application. Most importantly, the demonstrated easiness and low mental load required in conforming one's breathing to the application support the assumptions of embodied attuning and entrainment. However, the design process and evaluation also shed light on the design of interactive applications in a much more general level. They illustrate how UI presentation elements may be designed in such a way that they become graspable as motor movements – indicating affordances for certain body activity (without any direct anthropomorphic pointers to the body). Multimodal interaction, in turn, should be seen as more dynamic and intimate phenomenon than just switching between input and output (see [14]). Embodied cognition is a promising conceptual framework for a broader view than the traditional, information processing based approach. The experiences in the pilot study encourage going even further in the exploration of the nature of interaction between a computer application and its human operator; the notion of extended mind [15] perhaps best corresponds to our observations in the sessions of the evaluation test. In the relaxation process, the functions of the application and bodily functions blend to each other.

Acknowledgements. This work is funded by Finnish Funding Agency for Technology and Innovation (TEKES), and the following partners: GE Healthcare Finland Ltd., Suunto Ltd., Sandvik Mining and Construction Ltd. and Bronto Skylift Ltd.

References

1. Bradt, J.: Music Entrainment for Breathing Regulation. In: Music, the Breath and Health: Advances in Integrative Music Therapy, pp. 11–19. Satchnote Press, New York (2009)
2. Clayton, M., Sager, R., Will, U.: In time with music: The concept of entrainment and its significance for ethnomusicology. ESEM CounterPoint 1, 1–82 (2004)
3. Leman, M.: Embodied Music Cognition and Mediation Technology. MIT Press, Cambridge (2008)
4. Zentner, M.R., Eerola, T.: Rhythmic engagement with music in infancy. PNAS 107(13), 5768–5773 (2010)
5. Barlow, S.M., Finan, D.S., Park, S.: Sensorimotor entrainment of respiratory and orofacial systems in humans. In: Maassen, B., Kent, R., Peters, H. (eds.) Speech motor control, pp. 211–224. Oxford University Press, New York (2007)

6. Lucinia, D., Malacarnea, M., Solarob, N., Businc, S., Pagania, M.: Complementary medicine for the management of chronic stress: superiority of active versus passive techniques. Journal of Hypertension 27, 2421–2428 (2009)
7. Gavish, B.: Device-guided breathing in the home setting: Technology, performance and clinical outcomes. Biological Psychology 84, 150–156 (2010)
8. Wikipedia contributors: Wii Fit. In Wikipedia: The Free Encyclopedia, http://en.wikipedia.org/wiki/Wii_Fit (retrieved June 1, 2011)
9. Iacoboni, M.: Imitation, empathy, and mirror neurons. Annual Review of Psychology 60(1), 653–670 (2009)
10. Kohler, E., Keysers, C., Umiltá, M., Fogassi, L., Gallese, V., Rizzolatti, G.: Hearing sounds, understanding actions: action representation in mirror neurons. Science 297, 846–848 (2002)
11. Pirhonen, A.: Analysis of the concept of redundancy concerning the design of multimodal combinations of output-elements. In: Werner, B. (ed.) Proceedings in the 3rd Asia Pacific Computer Human Interaction, APCHI 1998, Shonan Village Center, Japan, July 15-17, pp. 273–278. IEEE, Los Alamitos (1998)
12. Johnson, M.: The body in the mind: The bodily basis of meaning, imagination, and reason. University of Chicago Press, Chicago (1987)
13. NASA: Task Load Index (TLX), http://human-factors.arc.nasa.gov/groups/TLX/ (accesses 5/5/2011)
14. Tuuri, K., Pirhonen, A., Hoggan, E.: Some severe deficiencies of the input-output HCI-paradigm and their influence on practical design. In: Norros, L., Koskinen, H., Salo, L., Savioja, P. (eds.) Proceedings of the European conference on Cognitive Ergonomics (ECCE 2009), Designing beyond the product – understanding activity and user experience in ubiquitous environments, Helsinki, Finland, September 30-October 2, pp. 363–369. VTT (Technical Research Centre of Finland), Helsinki (2009)
15. Clark, A.: Supersizing the mind: Embodiment, action, and cognitive extension. Oxford University Press, Oxford (2008)

Equal Intensity Contours for Whole-Body Vibrations Compared with Vibrations Cross-Modally Matched to Isophones

Sebastian Merchel, M. Ercan Altinsoy, and Maik Stamm

Chair of Communication Acoustics, Dresden University of Technology, Germany
sebastian.merchel@tu-dresden.de

Abstract. In this study, two experiments were conducted to determine the curves of equal intensity perception for sinusoidal vertical whole-body vibrations (WBV) of seated subjects over the frequency range from 10 Hz to 250 Hz. Vibrations were presented to subjects using a flat hard seat. In total, 10 participants were asked to match the intensity of different vibrations, using a method of adjustment. The obtained contours were compared with the threshold of vibration and to vibrations cross-modally matched to tones from isophones.

The shapes of the equal intensity contours in the present study show reasonable agreement with the contours from other studies despite the use of different methodologies and experimental questions. The contours show a characteristic similar to the perception threshold. No dependency of vibration magnitude on the shape of the contours was found in the applied dynamic range. However, large inter-individual variations were observed. The results imply that vibration curves that are cross-modally matched to isophones show similar characteristics.

Keywords: Equal Intensity Contour, Whole-Body Vibration, Isophone, Audio-Tactile Perception, Cross-Modality Matching.

1   Introduction

In a previous study [1], pure tones from isophones were cross-modally matched to vertical sinusoidal whole-body vibrations. It was hypothesized that the resulting vibrations are perceived with equal intensity. The present study investigates whether those contours coincide with curves of equal intensity perception for vertical sinusoidal whole-body vibrations.

Earlier studies have determined equivalent comfort contours for vertical sinusoidal whole-body vibrations mainly in the context of health risk estimation. Thus, only high vibration magnitudes and low frequencies have been investigated. A review can be found in Griffin [2]. The overall shape of the equivalent comfort contours is somewhat consistent between most of these studies: above 5 Hz the contours rise with increasing frequency. However, these contours represent discomfort or annoyance from whole-body vibrations. It is questionable if (dis-)comfort or annoyance can be compared to perceived vibration intensity.

E.W. Cooper et al. (Eds.): HAID 2011, LNCS 6851, pp. 71–80, 2011.

Few studies exist that measure vibrations close to the perception threshold or for frequencies above 100 Hz. Therefore, equal intensity contours will be measured for low magnitudes between 10 Hz and 250 Hz.

In an aim to compare the equal intensity contours with the perception threshold for sinusoidal vertical whole-body vibrations, threshold curves from various laboratories [3,4,5,6,7,8] were obtained and are summarized in Figure 1. The shapes of the threshold contours are similar. An overall trend of increasing threshold with increasing frequency is found over the range from 5 Hz to 300 Hz. However, Miwa [3] and Parson & Griffin [4] measured lower thresholds, particularly at lower frequencies. Different body postures or body support might explain some variability between studies in this frequency range. For example, the surface of the seat used by Morioka & Griffin [5] was contoured (to provide contact with the ischial tuberosities) and approximately half the size of the flat seats used in other studies, which themselves also provided contact with the thighs. The absence of contact with the thighs might reduce sensitivity to low-frequency vibrations. Differences between studies might also be partially explained by different psycho-physical methods. For example, Miwa [3], Bellmann [6], Stamm et al. [7] and Merchel & Leppin [8] used different adaptive n-interval forced choice methods, whereas Parsons & Griffin [4] and Morioka & Griffin [5] employed a 'yes-no' method.

Two frequency regions can be separated and fitted by 1st order regressions. At lower frequencies, the perception threshold increases slightly by approximately 1.3 dB per octave. Above 150 Hz, the increase climbs up to 6.5 dB per octave. No prediction can be made outside of the shown frequency range. The regression curves must be interpreted carefully since few measurement points are available at higher frequencies. However, Morioka and Griffin [5] reported a significant increase for frequencies above 200 Hz. It can be seen that the threshold curve from ISO 2631:1989 [9], which was removed from the revised ISO 2631:2003 [10], does not represent the data well. Thus, the fitted curves will be used for comparison later in this study.

2   Experiment

Two experiments were conducted to determine the curves of equal intensity perception of sinusoidal vertical whole-body vibrations for seated subjects. The subjects were asked to compare the intensity of a reference vibration with a test stimulus using a method of adjustment. In the first experiment, two curves determined using different reference frequencies were obtained. One reference frequency was selected and used in the second experiment to determine equal intensity curves over a wider dynamic range.

2.1   Setup

Whole-body vibrations were generated vertically using an electro-dynamic shaker. The subject was seated on a flat hard wooden seat (460 mm x 460 mm) with

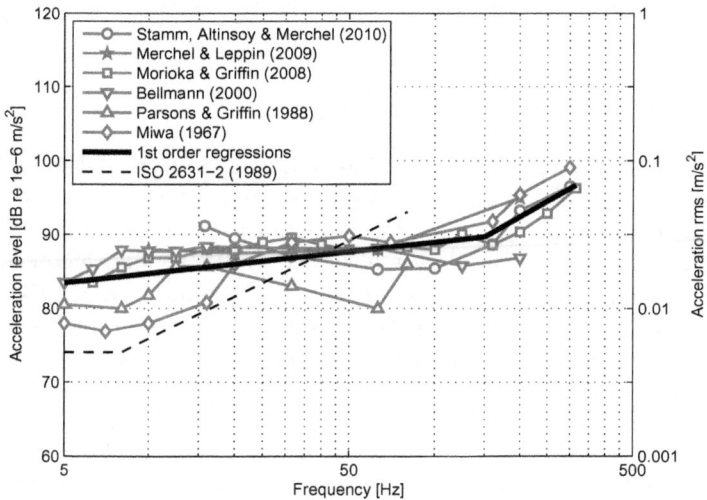

Fig. 1. Perception threshold for vertical sinusoidal whole-body vibrations from various laboratories in comparison to the threshold from ISO 2631:1989 [9]. 1st order regressions were fitted to the data below and above 150 Hz.

both feet on the ground. There was no backrest. The transfer characteristic of the vibrating chair is strongly dependent on the individual person [11]. This phenomenon is referred to as the body related transfer function (BRTF). The BRTF of each subject was individually monitored using a vibration pad (B&K Type 4515B) and a Sinus Harmonie quadro measuring board and individually compensated using inverse filters in Matlab.

For higher frequencies, the vibration chair can emit acoustic noise. Pink noise was presented at 74 dB(A) to acoustically mask the noises emitted by the chair. In addition, unwanted auditory feedback possibly delivered through bone conduction will be masked as well. The audio signal was delivered through an external Hammerfall DSP Multiface sound card, amplified by a Phone-Amp G93 and reproduced through a set of Sennheiser HDA 200 closed dynamic headphones.

The participant was able to control the amplitude of the vibration using a rotary knob that was infinitely adjustable and did not possess any visual indicators (Griffin Technology, PowerMate).

2.2   Subjects

Ten subjects (6 male and 4 female) voluntarily participated in both experiments. Most of the participants were students between 19 years and 27 years old (mean 23 years). The participants had masses between 62 kg and 85 kg (mean 71 kg) and indicated to have no hearing or spinal damage.

The subjects were instructed to sit upright with comfortable posture, their hands on their thighs and both feet flat on the ground. Additional plates were used to adjust the height of the feet until the thighs were approximately horizontal and level with the seat.

2.3   Stimuli and Experimental Design

Seven vibration frequencies over a wide frequency range (10 Hz, 20 Hz, 50 Hz, 100 Hz, 150 Hz, 200 Hz and 250 Hz) were selected for the experiments. In the first experiment, two frequencies were selected as reference frequencies (20 Hz and 100 Hz) with a fixed acceleration level of 110 dB. The reference vibration was presented for one second followed by a 0.5 s break. Afterwards, one of the test frequencies was reproduced for one second. The order of the test frequencies was completely randomized. All vibration signals were faded in and out using half a hanning window of 50 ms flanks. Reference and test stimuli were marked visually using the experimental interface controlled by Matlab. The task of the subject was to adaptively adjust the perceived intensity of the test vibration to the perceived intensity of the reference vibration using the rotary knob. The test frequency was adjustable with a minimum step size of 0.25 dB. The initial acceleration level of the test whole-body vibration was 90 ± 5 dB (a random offset was used for each trial). A low initial acceleration was necessary because the dynamic range of vibration perception is small and a high level of vibration may cause discomfort. This sequence was automatically repeated until the participant was satisfied with his/her match. The subject was free to take as much time as necessary to make the proper adjustments. The total duration of the experiment varied between participants and took between 25 and 35 minutes to match both reference vibrations with all 7 test vibrations (including a familiarization phase in the beginning). For the 100 Hz reference condition, each match was repeated three times for all participants to check intra-individual repeatability.

In the second experiment, a reference frequency of 20 Hz was used with various acceleration levels ranging close to the perceptual threshold until moderately strong values (100 dB, 105 dB, 110 dB, 115 dB and 120 dB). The experimental design was identical to the first experiment. The total duration of the experiment varied between 35 minutes and 45 minutes, depending on the individual subject.

3   Results and Discussion

3.1   Experiment 1 – Different Reference Frequencies

Figure 2 shows the individual equal intensity contours for vertical sinusoidal whole-body vibrations for all subjects using a reference frequency of 100 Hz with an acceleration level of 110 dB. As expected, the results show small deviations at the reference frequency. The individual contours match well toward higher frequencies, but increasing inter-individual differences are found toward lower frequencies. The intra-individual standard deviations (not plotted here) are comparatively small, in the range between 1 dB and 3 dB independent of frequency, which indicates good repeatability.

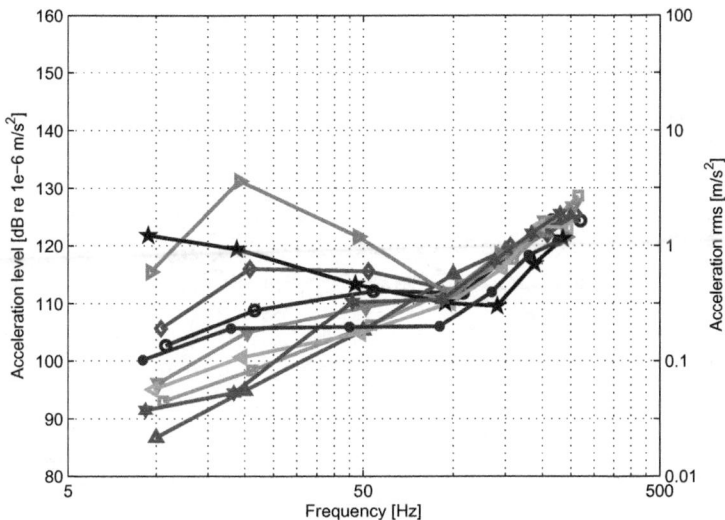

Fig. 2. Individual equal intensity contours for vertical sinusoidal whole-body vibrations for all subjects using a reference frequency of 100 Hz with an acceleration level of 110 dB

In Figure 3, individual equal intensity contours for a reference frequency of 20 Hz with an acceleration level of 110 dB are plotted. The measured individual contours agree for low frequencies but show considerable differences toward higher frequencies. The amount of variation is comparable to the data shown in Figure 2. It can be concluded that contours of equally perceived intensity are highly subject dependent. This dependency could be explained with strong inter-individual differences in the perception threshold as found in [8]. However, no threshold data exist for the participants in the present study.

To compare the results, the mean was calculated for both conditions. The averaged intensity contours are plotted in Figure 4 with inter-individual standard deviations. The mean values increase depending on the frequency from 10 Hz to 250 Hz. The inter-individual standard deviations increase with increasing distance from the reference frequencies. However, the averaged contours show reasonable agreement. Thus, the 20 Hz reference stimulus was used with various levels in the following experiment. The averaged contours should be interpreted and used carefully because of the high inter-individual deviations.

3.2   Experiment 2 – Different Magnitudes

Figure 5 shows the averaged equal intensity contours for vertical sinusoidal whole-body vibrations using a reference frequency of 20 Hz with acceleration levels of 100 dB, 105 dB, 110 dB, 115 dB and 120 dB. The contours are almost parallel at lower frequencies and show some deviations at higher frequencies. This finding can be explained by the increasing distance to the reference stimu-

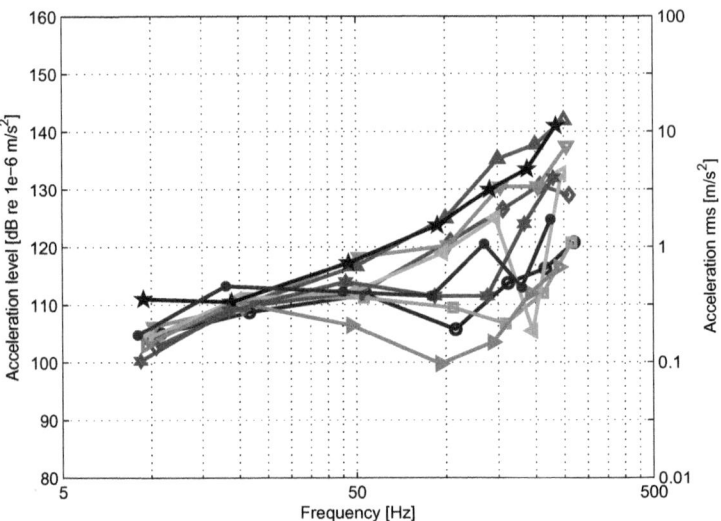

Fig. 3. Individual equal intensity contours for vertical sinusoidal whole-body vibrations for all subjects using a reference frequency of 20 Hz with an acceleration level of 110 dB

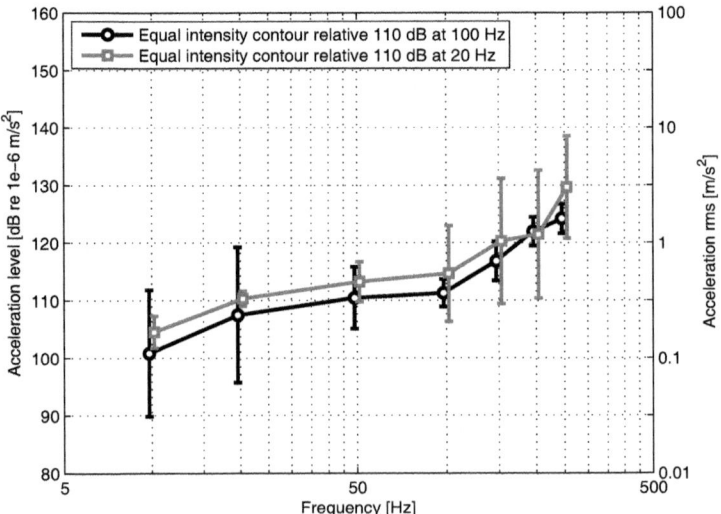

Fig. 4. Comparison between averaged equal intensity contours for vertical sinusoidal whole-body vibrations using a reference frequency of 20 Hz and 100 Hz with an acceleration level of 110 dB

lus. Two subjects in particular showed inconsistencies for higher test frequencies (see Figure 3). The inter-individual standard deviations increase with increasing frequency. The variations are independent of vibration magnitude and compa-

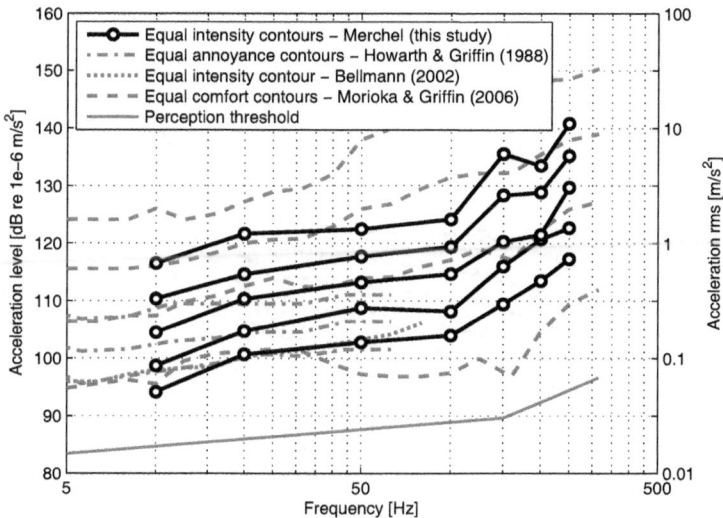

Fig. 5. Comparison of equal perception contours for sinusoidal vertical whole-body vibrations from different laboratories

rable to the results shown in Figure 4; they will not be plotted here for a better overview. The averaged contours increase depending on the frequency from 10 Hz to 250 Hz. The slope is shallow up to 100 Hz and steepens for higher frequencies up to 250 Hz. The curves increase above 100 Hz with approximately 9 dB per octave. The general shape is comparable with the averaged perception threshold, which is also plotted in Figure 5 for comparison.

Few studies have investigated equal perception contours for low magnitudes of vibration and/or a broad frequency range. Bellmann [6] measured an equal intensity contour between 5 Hz and 80 Hz using an adaptive two-interval forced choice procedure. A reference frequency of 20 Hz at 100 dB was used, which corresponds to the weakest reference stimuli of the present study. The resulting contour is plotted in Figure 5 for comparison and shows reasonable agreement.

Morioka & Griffin [12] used magnitude estimation to determine judgements of *discomfort* caused by vertical vibrations over a wide frequency and dynamic range. Equal (dis-)comfort contours were then calculated from the data. The resulting curves are plotted in Figure 5 for comparison. Note that the bottom and top contour in the plot do not predominantly represent measured vibrations but are determined by extrapolation. The contours show a similar tendency as in the present study, but no pronounced break at 100 Hz. The data from Morioka & Griffin [12] confirm that the contours are similar to the perception threshold for low sensation magnitudes. However, Morioka & Griffin [12] found a dependence of the magnitude on the shape of the equal comfort contours. This result differs somewhat from the present findings but might be explained by the different experimental question (discomfort versus intensity) and the solely low acceleration levels used in the present study. The results at low magnitudes in

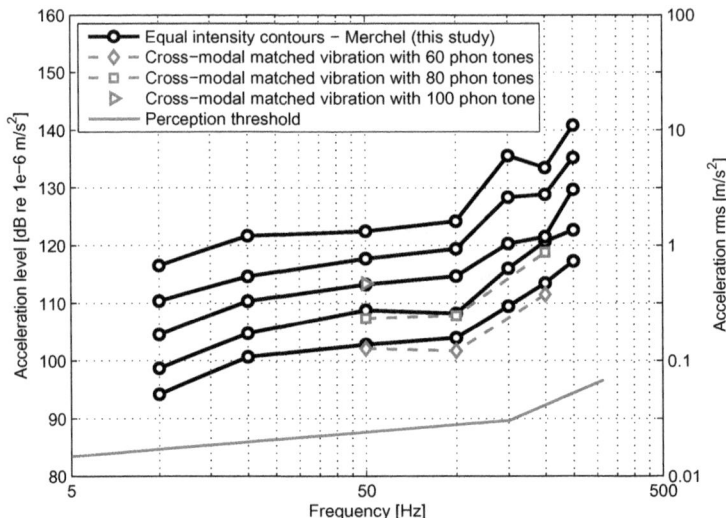

Fig. 6. Comparison of equal intensity contours for sinusoidal vertical whole-body vibrations (present study) with cross-modally matched vibrations with tones from equal loudness contours [1]

the present study deviate in general from literature using higher accelerations (e.g., health risk, annoyance or discomfort curves; see Griffin [2] for an overview), which show steeper slopes.

Earlier data can be found in Howarth & Griffin [13], who used an acoustical reference stimulus (1/3 octave band noise centered at 1 kHz) to measure *annoyance* caused by vibration using a method of magnitude estimation. Only frequencies up to 63 Hz were measured with a small dynamic range. Interestingly, the resulting annoyance contours are consistent with the equal intensity contours from the present study as illustrated in Figure 5.

Merchel et al. [1] hypothesized that cross-modally matched vibrations with tones from equal loudness contours might be similar to equal intensity contours for whole-body vibrations like the ones measured in the present study. Figure 6 shows the results from both studies for comparison. The data is consistent between experiments. This finding suggests that equal intensity contours could be used to predict cross-modal matching between the loudness of sounds and the perceived intensity of whole-body vibrations. Most participants reported that intensity matching within a modality, which reduces experimental time and complexity, is a much easier task than matching across modalities.

Merchel et al. [1] found that an increase of 20 phon in the loudness level resulted in a 5 dB - 6 dB increase in the matched acceleration level (at loudness levels greater than 40 phon). A 20 phon increase in the loudness level corresponds to a quadruplication of perceived loudness. It might thus be assumed that the perceived intensity of sinusoidal vertical whole-body vibrations is approximately doubled through a 2.5 dB - 3 dB increase in acceleration level. This trend may only be true for the investigated frequency and dynamic range and could be tested with a magnitude estimation experiment in a further study.

4   Summary and Outlook

In this study, contours of equally perceived intensity were determined for vertical sinusoidal whole-body vibrations. The following results were obtained:
  - The shapes of the equal intensity contours in the present study show reasonable agreement with the contours from other studies despite the use of different methodologies and experimental questions.
  - Small intra-individual and large inter-individual variations were observed.
  - Contours from cross-modally matched vibrations with tones from equal loudness contours show a similar shape if compared to the measured equal intensity contours for whole-body vibrations of the present study.

Future research should investigate even lower vibration magnitudes than the present study. Another open question is the variability between subjects, which remains to be explained.

Acknowledgements. The authors wish to thank Prof. U. Jekosch for her support and informative discussions.

References

1. Merchel, S., Altinsoy, M.E.: Cross-Modality Matching of Loudness and Perceived Intensity of Whole-Body Vibrations. In: Nordahl, R., Serafin, S., Fontana, F., Brewster, S. (eds.) HAID 2010. LNCS, vol. 6306, pp. 1–9. Springer, Heidelberg (2010)
2. Griffin, M.J.: Handbook of Human Vibration. Academic Press, London (1990)
3. Miwa, T.: Evaluation Methods for Vibration Effect, Part 1: Measurements of Threshold and Equal Sensation Contours of Whole-Body for Vertical and Horizontal Vibrations. Industrial Health 5, 183–205 (1967)
4. Parsons, K.C., Griffin, M.J.: Whole-Body Vibration Perception Thresholds. J. Sound Vib. 121, 237–258 (1988)
5. Morioka, M., Griffin, M.J.: Absolute Thresholds for the Perception of Fore-and-Aft, Lateral, and Vertical Vibration at the Hand, the Seat, and the Foot. J. Sound Vib. 314, 357–370 (2008)
6. Bellmann, M.: Perception of Whole-Body Vibrations: From Basic Experiments to Effects of Seat and Steering-Wheel Vibrations on the Passenger's Comfort Inside Vehicles, Ph.D. Thesis, Carl von Ossietzky Universität Oldenburg (2002)
7. Stamm, M., Altinsoy, M.E., Merchel, S.: Frequenzwahrnehmung von Ganzkörperschwingungen im Vergleich zur auditiven Wahrnehmung I und II. In: Proceedings of DAGA 2010, Berlin, Germany (2010)
8. Merchel, S., Leppin, A., Altinsoy, M.E.: The Influence of Whole Body Vibrations on Loudness Perception. In: ICSV 16, Kraków, Poland (2009)
9. International Organization of Standardisation: ISO 2631-2:1989 Evaluation of Human Exposure to Whole-Body Vibration – Part 2: Continuous and Shock-Induced Vibrations in Buildings (1 Hz to 80 Hz), Geneva (1989)

10. International Organization of Standardisation: ISO 2631-2:2003 Evaluation of Human Exposure to Whole-Body Vibration – Part 2: Vibrations in Buildings (1 Hz to 80 Hz), Geneva (2003)
11. Altinsoy, M.E., Merchel, S.: BRTF - Body Related Transfer Functions for Whole-Body Vibration Reproduction Systems. In: DAGA, Rotterdam, Netherlands (2009)
12. Morioka, M., Griffin, M.J.: Magnitude-Dependence of Equivalent Comfort Contours for Fore-and-Aft, Lateral and Vertical Whole-Body Vibration. J. Sound Vib. 298, 755–772 (2006)
13. Howarth, H.V.C., Griffin, M.J.: The Frequency Dependence of Subjective Reaction to Vertical and Horizontal Whole-Body Vibration at Low Magnitudes. J. Acoust. Soc. Am. 83(4), 1406–1413 (1988)

Spinlock: A Single-Cue Haptic and Audio PIN Input Technique for Authentication

Andrea Bianchi[1], Ian Oakley[2], and Dong Soo Kwon[1]

[1] KAIST, Daejeon, Korea
[2] Madera ITI, University of Madeira, Funchal, Portugal
andrea@kaist.ac.kr, ian@uma.pt, kwonds@kaist.ac.kr

Abstract. Authentication in public spaces is inherently exposed to observation attacks in which passwords are stolen by the simple act of watching the data input process. Addressing this issue are systems that secure authentication input via PINs or passwords that rely on sets of relatively unobservable tactile or audio cues. However, although secure, such systems typically invoke high levels of cognitive load in their users which is instantiated in lengthy authentication times and high error rates and most likely due to significant cognitive demands in terms of processing, mapping or recalling non visual information. To address this issue this paper introduces Spinlock, a novel authentication technique based on repeated presentation, recognition and enumeration of a single, simple invisible cue (audio or haptic), rather than a set of structured stimuli. This approach maintains the security but avoids the complexity of previous systems. A prototype illustrating this concept is described as well as a study comparing modalities and gauging overall levels of performance, usability and security. The results show that authentication with Spinlock is faster and less error prone than previous non-visual systems, while maintaining a similar security level. Limitations and future work are discussed.

Keywords: Authentication, haptic and audio PIN, mobile.

1 Introduction

Users' interaction with PIN-entry interfaces situated in public spaces is inherently observable by third parties. While this is acceptable in many situations, such as while interacting with information kiosks, it is problematic during confidential interactions such as PIN entry at bank ATMs or public password entry on mobile devices. In these cases, the observable nature of the input device becomes a weakness that can be subjected to observation attacks, both in person (a technique known as shoulder surfing) and via appropriately positioned video recording equipment (a camera attack). These risks are significant – ATM fraud in the USA is estimated to run to 60 million USD per year [1] – and have been comprehensively discussed in the research community [2].

In order to create observation resistant data entry techniques, recent research has explored the use of invisible cues, such as audio or haptics, as an alternative input/output method to support PIN entry in public terminals [e.g. 3, 4]. Fundamentally, the argument underlying this work is that the highly physical or

E.W. Cooper et al. (Eds.): HAID 2011, LNCS 6851, pp. 81–90, 2011.

Fig. 1. Inserting a PIN in the Spinlock application (left) and the Spinlock hardware setup (right) - an Apple Ipod Touch and a Shake SK6 unit for generating vibration stimuli

proximate nature of invisible cues (touch or audio through headphones) makes it more difficult for observers to intercept key information both in person and via recording equipment –that observing haptic/audio information is more challenging than observing traditional PIN entry activities, such as key presses.

Current research supports this suggestion [e.g. 3, 4]. However, the use of these cues is not without its limitations. Most importantly, while harder for a third party to observe, a set of invisible cues (often in the form of tactons [5]) is also more challenging for a user to accurately perceive, process and interpret. Secure haptic data entry tasks, for instance, have typically resulted in high levels of cognitive load expressed empirically through lengthy task completion times and high error rates [3, 4]. The work described in this paper aims to retain the observation-resistant property of haptic and audio cues - the threat model considered in this work is malicious observation of PIN entry in person and via recording equipment in a public space. However, this paper aims to mitigate the cognitive effort required to interpret such non-traditional password cues. It does this by presenting the design of Spinlock, a system based on the repeated display of a single, simple and easy to recognize cue, rather than a set of structured invisible stimuli [e.g., 3]. It also explicitly compares audio with haptic cues and presents a discussion of the differences observed.

The remainder of this paper is structured as follows: a literature review; a description of the conceptual structure of the security system and the details of a prototype for mobile phones that instantiates it; a user study incorporating usability and security evaluations; a discussion of the results and speculations for future work.

2   Related Work

Researchers have explored a wide range of haptic and audio techniques for PIN entry. Most of early work in this area used a multi-modal approach, combining the rich visual modality of graphical or textual passwords with haptic or audible cues. For example, in early work on this topic Malek et al. [6] described haptic passwords that used pressure-based input as a hidden channel to obfuscate entry of an otherwise graphical password. In this system users drew a password composed of lines connecting points on a grid, and the pressure applied during drawing was used as supplementary information to compose the password.

More recently, both Sasamoto et al [4] and de Luca et al [7] described data entry techniques based on the combination of observable visual input modified via a users perception of unobservable tactile cues in the form of directional strokes applied to the skin or the vibrations of a mobile device. Although promising, these approaches require users invest significant cognitive resources in order to map known actions to sensed haptic stimuli, or rely on the user's perception and recognition of hidden haptic cues in order to transform their observable input. Such mental mappings are not trivial and lead to lengthy authentication times and high error rates: for instance in Sasamoto's Undercover system median task completion times are reported to be 25-45 seconds, with error rates of between 26%-52% [4].

In contrast to this multi-modal approach, Bianchi et al. [3] proposed a uni-modal haptic password based on selecting a sequence of tactons in much the same way as numbers are selected on a regular keypad. To secure against observation, the tactons were randomized over the keys between selections. The task in this system is simply to recognize and select haptic cues and the authors argue this simplicity should result in lower levels of cognitive load (and correspondingly improved task completion times and error rates) when compared to multi-modal approaches. Evaluations of a number of system variations, including an audio entry systems that works analogously to the haptic version [8, 9], support this claim (authentication in less than 20 seconds, with 7% mean error rate) as does highly related work by Kuber and Yu [10], in which a similar concept is instantiated based on spatially varying cues rendered on Braille cells explored by the fingertips. However, a disadvantage of such systems is that they require users to accurately select particular haptic cues from a stimulus set, a challenging task when sets exceed 3 or 4 items in size [e.g. 3, 8, 9, 11]. Issues of learning and retention of tactons are also poorly understood - from the perspective of human cognitive limits, it is currently unclear how scalable and reliable the concept of a purely haptic password really is [11]. These issues place doubts on the viability of these recognition-based approaches.

On the other hand, work on audio authentication has typically focused on identity recognition and used speech as an auxiliary input modality in combination with other biometric techniques (e.g., lip sync, fingerprints, face recognition) [12, 13]. Although these systems do provide stronger multi-factor authentication based on orthogonal data sources, they do not attempt to offer a direct solution to the observation attack; voice can be easily recorded in public spaces using directional microphones and such systems can be sensitive to replay attacks utilizing playback of such data.

The work in this paper addresses these issues. Its contribution is the design of a PIN entry system that relies on simple uni-modal haptic or audio cues, but that does not require users to learn or distinguish among a large set of distinct stimuli, nor use the audio or haptic modality as a compliment to other input. It achieves this via the rapid, repeated display of a single, brief and distinctive cue in response to user input. By counting the number of displayed cues (either haptic or audio), users can enter structured data. This design seeks to retain the advantages of non-visual uni-modal PIN entry while sidestepping issues of learning and recognizing a stimulus set.

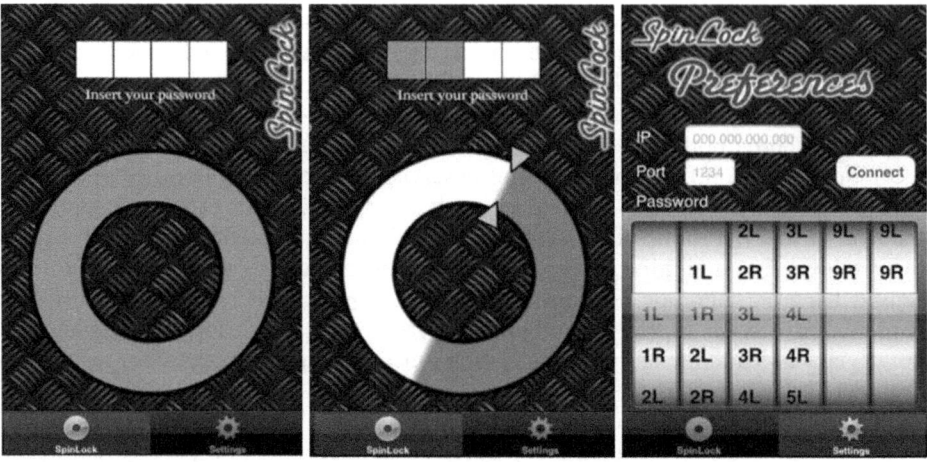

Fig. 2. The Spinlock graphical user interface: whilst idle (left), during the user interaction with two PIN items entered (center) and the settings screen showing user password (right)

3   Design and Implementation of the Spinlock PIN Entry System

The Spinlock prototype is based on the dial-lock of a safe. In such systems, PINs are composed of a sequence of numbers and a direction of motion (clockwise/right or anti-clockwise/left), which must alternate. For example, in a dial marked with 10 numbers, a four-item PIN could take the form of the following rotations: 2-left, 8-right, 5-left, and 7-right. Spinlock is based on a similar interaction with two key differences. Firstly, the requirement to alternate directions is removed (via the provision of widget deselection, an additional input delimiter). Secondly, rather than moving to a number marked on a dial, users count the number of audio or haptic cues delivered during their input. Upon termination, the direction of their motion and the number of cues they experienced constitute the PIN item sent to the system.

For example, to enter the password listed above, users would input leftward rotation until two audio or haptic cues were experienced, followed by rightward motion for a count of eight cues, leftward for five and finally rightward for seven. Although this password features alternating directions, this is not a requirement for the Spinlock system - input can also be delimited by deselection of the control widget.

In order to remain resistant to observation the spatial distance users must travel between cue presentations is randomized (among 7 possible distances, 12° apart from each other, ranging from 36° to 120°) after every cue. The goal of this manipulation is to increase the resistance of the system to attack via visual observation. It decouples the distance that the Spinlock dial is rotated from a direct correspondence with the data that is input.

To explore the validity of this design, Spinlock was implemented for the Apple iPhone and iPod Touch devices (Figures 1 and 2). The touch screen was used for input. Users interact with the system by selecting the edge of the circular dial widget (4cm diameter) and dragging a cursor around its rim. The wheel color changes to indicate the direction of motion and as users move brief haptic or audio clicks are played. The audio output is provided by standard earphones connected to the device's audio jack, while the tactile output is delivered via a matchbox sized SHAKE SK6 device capable of delivering a wide range of tactile cues [14]. The connection to the SK6 is achieved via a link to a PC (Wi-Fi) that communicates to the SHAKE device via Bluetooth. The SHAKE was manually mounted on the back of the phone with Velcro fasteners. The audio cues used in the system take the form of 113 ms audio *beeps* (Mono, 44100Hz, stored in a *wav* file). Analogously, the haptic cues are represented by sharp 50 ms vibro-tactile *buzzes*. These two cues were select to be short and distinctive via iterative, subjective testing by the authors during system development. Users are able to cancel a PIN entry at any time by shaking the device, a gesture captured from the built-in accelerometers.

The Spinlock GUI is composed of two screens, one to customize settings and the other to enter PINs. The first screen allows users to specify the length of the PIN (4-6 digits) and the direction-count pairs that compose it (numbers from 1 to 10 in either the clockwise or anti-clockwise direction). Connections to the host PC (via sockets for communication to the SHAKE device and data logging) are also managed on this screen. The PIN entry screen shows the input dial and a bar of colored rectangles which indicate PIN entry progress - grey for the number of PIN items entered, green for a correct complete PIN and red for a failed complete PIN.

4 Evaluation

Spinlock was evaluated with a user study. The goals were to compare performance between the two display modalities, to compare performance among PINs of varying complexity and to determine the resistance of the technique to observation attacks conducted via audio-visual recording equipment. Correspondingly, the study incorporated four conditions derived from two binary independent variables: modality and PIN complexity. The two modalities considered were *haptic* and *audio* cues, while the PIN complexity was manipulated by altering the data input range. This was achieved by varying the maximum number of cues that each PIN item could be composed of from five (*short:* each PIN item involved counting a number of cues in the range of between one and five inclusive) to ten (*long:* PIN items were from one to ten inclusive). Since each PIN item also includes an orthogonal binary direction component (left/right), the *short* PIN encompasses 10^4 possible combinations, equal to a standard 4 digit numerical PIN in terms of the level of security it provides against a brute-force (or PIN guessing) attack. The *long* PIN has 20^4 possible combinations, a significantly increased figure.

The study itself had a repeated measures design and involved 12 participants (seven male, five female with age between 22 and 30 years) each completing all four experimental conditions. PIN complexity was balanced among participants, with six completing each of the two possible orders. Modality was balanced within each PIN complexity block, such that three participants always started with haptics and three with audio. Each condition required participants make 15 successful PIN entries. The first five were considered practice and analysis restricted to subsequent interactions. Consequently data analysis took place on 40 correct PIN entries per user. As with most current ATM systems, each PIN was composed of four items so a total of 480 complete correct PIN entries and 1920 individual data inputs were examined. Erroneous input after completion of the practice trials was also analyzed.

The experiment was conducted in an empty office with participants seated in front of a desktop computer. After filling basic demographics and reading experimental instructions, they were shown the mobile device and provided with a randomly generated PIN in written form (either *short* or *long* depending on the order condition) and an experimenter demonstrated how to correctly enter a PIN. Participants were then given the opportunity to freely explore the system for a maximum of five minutes before the formal conditions commenced. All input took place on the mobile device, but experimental data was streamed to the desktop PC, which also displayed a window indicating the number of successful PIN entries required to complete the current condition. After completing one haptic and one audio condition, participants received a new randomly generated PIN (either *short* or *long* to complement their previous PIN) and used this for the remainder of the study. The experiment took 30-45 minutes in total.

Experimental measures were successful PIN entry time, error rate and the number of times users canceled a PIN entry process. Participants also completed a NASA TLX questionnaire directly after each condition. Data logging captured fine grained data relating to all user interactions. Finally, audio and video of the participants' hands and the mobile device running the experimental software were captured with a Sony camcorder mounted on a tripod and positioned directly over their shoulders.

5   Results

Experimental data are shown in Figure 3. All data were tested using two-way repeated measures ANOVAs. The authentication time performance attained a significant main effect of modality (F (11, 1)=9.08, p=0.012) and PIN complexity (F (11, 1)=13.8, p=0.003), but the interaction between these two variables was not significant (F (121, 1)=0.28, p=0.6). Authentication errors showed significant effect of modality

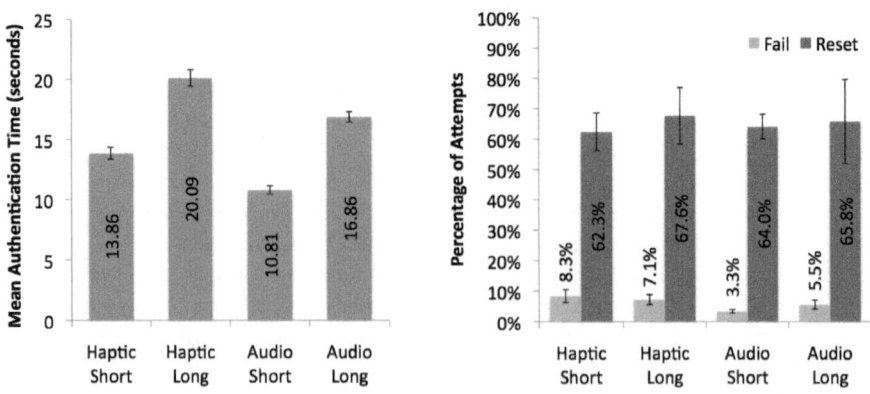

Fig. 3. Mean authentication time (left); mean percentage of failed trails and resets events (right). Bars show Std Error.

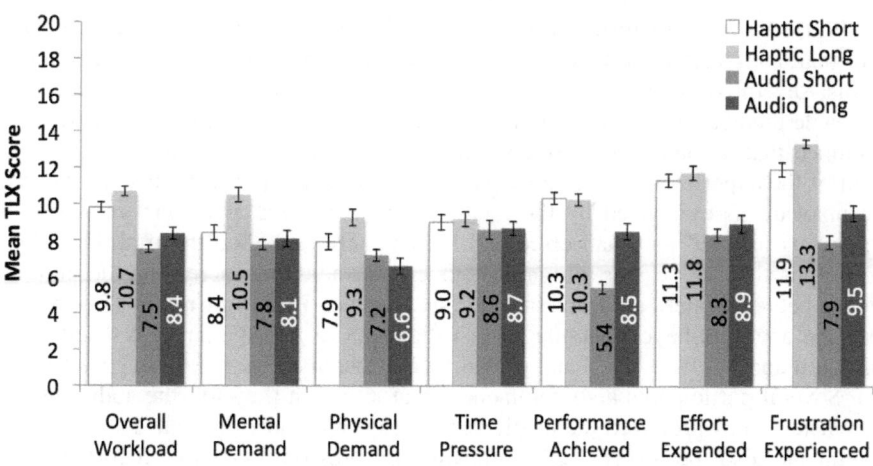

Fig. 4. NASA TLX ratings: higher scores show higher workload. Bars show Std Error

(F (11,1)=5.8, p=0.034) but not PIN complexity (F (11,1)=1.44, p=0.256) or interaction among the two (F (121,1)=0.66, p=0.433). Canceled PIN entries (resets) showed no significant variations across PIN complexity or modality (F (11,1)=2.65, p=0.13; F (11,1)=0.81, p=0.38). Finally, the two-way ANOVA on the overall workload of the TLX (Figure 4) showed a significant effect of modality (F (11,1)=15.23, p=0.002) but not PIN complexity (F (11,1)=3.7, p=0.081).

6 Discussion

This experimental work in this paper sought to explore how performance with the Spinlock system varied between haptic and audio cue presentation modalities and between PINs composed of more or less complex cues. The results clearly showed that participants found the haptic modality more challenging: significant differences were observed in the mean PIN entry times, failed authentication rates and overall workload. One possible explanation for this is system latency: the haptic effects were delivered on a wirelessly connected device while the audio cues were triggered *in-situ*. Although the impact of this cannot be determined by the current study, future work on this topic need more carefully control latency in the display of haptic cues.

PIN complexity, on the other hand, resulted in increased task completion times, but had no significant effect on other metrics. The increased time is unsurprising in this case: compared to the *short* complexity condition, participants had to make larger input strokes in the *long* complexity condition. The fact that the increase in complexity did not result in increases in the error rate or levels of workload strongly suggests that the task of counting the haptic and audio cues is easy to understand, effective and scalable. This is an encouraging result.

Analyzing the erroneous PIN entry trials also provided valuable insights into participant performance. In these trials, no errors of direction of travel were made and 82% of error trials involved a mistake in only one PIN item (from the four composing each PIN). Also, the majority of errors (78%) involved entering digits one higher or lower than the target item. Comments by participants provided a feasible explanation for this; several spontaneously remarked that the randomly distributed nature of the cues made predicting the location of the final target challenging. In particular, several mentioned that unintentionally overshooting the target item was the most frustrating aspect of the experiment. That participants were typically aware of such errors, rather than unaware, is evidenced by the relatively high number of manual reset events - participants realized they had erred and immediately cancelled the trial. Participants also proposed strategies for mitigating this effect, including increasing the minimum spacing between cues, randomizing cue spacing per PIN item rather than per cue, accepting one item beyond the target as valid input (e.g. if the target is 4-left, accept both 4-left and 5-left as valid) and providing a mechanism for re-entering a single PIN item. Several participants also commented that although they felt the audio interface was "easier", they preferred the haptic version as it was more "private".

Spinlock also performs well compared to previous systems reported in the literature. For example, PhoneLock [9], an authentication system based on the recognition of a set of tactile or audio cues achieves mean authentication times and error rates of 18.7 seconds and 7% compared to the 15.4 seconds and 6% observed in the current study. Considering haptic performance alone, mean task time in the Spinlock system improves 30% over that reported in PhoneLock (16.9 seconds vs. 24.05 seconds). These results suggest that systems that rely on counting haptic cues may be more effective that those that rely on tactons, at least in some scenarios.

7 Security Analysis

By relying on the perception of non-visual cues Spinlock obfuscates its data input process - unlike keypad systems for PIN entry, simply looking at a user's hands whilst they are entering data does reveal the PIN contents. The randomization of spacing between the cues delivered by the system was intended to reinforce this and reduce the relationship between the user's observable input and the PIN item they enter. However, an analysis correlating PIN item entry time with PIN item number across all four experimental conditions was significant (r (28) = 0.87, p<0.001) indicating this manipulation was not fully successful and representing a security threat.

To gauge the severity of this threat, an expert with full knowledge of the Spinlock system performed an observation attack using the complete set of experimental videos taken from two randomly chosen participants (a total of 80 authentications using four PINS and both modality and complexity conditions). To facilitate the attack, the expert was provided with a table indicating mean selection times for each PIN item. The expert was unable to correctly deduce any of the four PINs studied and reported that determining a PIN from a single observation would be impossible. However, the repeated presentation of each PIN 20 times enabled trends to be ascertained. In particular, the expert performed well with PIN items with low digits (rapid trials) and was able to easily isolate (although not precisely ascertain) input relating to high digits. Audio cues from the camera's microphone were not reported to contain any useful information - even in the stable, quiet lab environment the attacker stated that neither the audio cues to the headphones or the vibrations to the SHAKE produced any environmentally audible noise.

8 Conclusions and Future Work

The contribution of this work is the presentation of a novel design for a haptic and audio PIN entry system. It combines the simplicity of previous approaches based on simply recognizing cues (rather than applying further mental mappings or transformations to the perceived information [e.g. 4, 6]) but avoids the overhead of requiring users to learn and recognize a large stimuli set [e.g. as in 3, 8, 9]. It achieves this by asking users to count, rather than accurately distinguish, the number of simple, identical haptic or audio cues that are delivered in response to their input.

A prototype instantiating this idea, Spinlock, was developed and a preliminary evaluation performed. The results show this approach has considerable promise and suggest it can reduce the high levels of cognitive load (and associated task times and error rates) observed in studies of previous non-visual PIN entry systems. The study also suggests fruitful avenues for future work, including potential revisions to the interaction design that provide better error prevention or recovery mechanisms and the need to address a security weakness to repeated observations through the development of improved randomization functions for stimuli presentation. Further empirical user studies and security analyses to validate such refinements are also required.

Acknowledgments. Partial support for this research was provided by the Fundação para a Ciência e a Tecnologia (Portuguese Foundation for Science and Technology) through the Carnegie Mellon | Portugal Program. We would also like to thank our experimental participants.

References

1. Giesen, L.: ATM fraud: Does it warrant the expense to fight it? Banking Strategies 82(6) (2006)
2. De Luca, A., Langheinrich, M., Hussmann, H.: Towards understanding ATM security: a field study of real world ATM use. In: Proceedings SOUPS 2010 (2010)
3. Bianchi, A., Oakley, I., Kwon, D.S.: The Secure Haptic Keypad: Design and Evaluation of a Tactile Password System. In: CHI 2010, pp. 1089–1092. ACM, New York (2010)
4. Sasamoto, H., Christin, N., Hayashi, E.: Undercover: authentication usable in front of prying eyes. In: Procs of CHI 2008, pp. 183–192. ACM, New York (2008)
5. Brewster, S.A., Brown, L.M.: Non-visual information display using tactons. In: Procs of CHI 2004 Extended Abstracts, pp. 787–788 (2004)
6. Malek, B., Orozco, M., Saddik, A.: Novel shoulder- surfing resistant haptic-based graphical password. In: Proceedings of EuroHaptics (2006)
7. De Luca, A., von Zezschwitz, E., Hußmann, H.: Vibrapass: secure authentication based on shared lies. In: Procs. of CHI 2009, pp. 913–916. ACM, New York (2009)

8. Bianchi, A., Oakley, I., Lee, J., Kwon, D.: The haptic wheel: design & evaluation of a tactile password system. In: Proceedings of CHI 2010, pp. 3625–3630. ACM, New York (2010)
9. Bianchi, A., Oakley, I., Kostakos, V., Kwon, D.: The Phone Lock: Audio and Haptic shoulder-surfing resistant PIN entry methods. In: Proc. of ACM TEI 2011. ACM, New York (2011)
10. Kuber, R., Yu, W.: Feasibility study of tactile-based authentication. International Journal of Human-Computer Studies 68(3), 158–181 (2010)
11. Brown, L.M., Brewster, S.A., Purchase, H.C.: Purchase, Multidimensional tactons for non-visual information presentation in mobile devices. In: Proc. of MobileHCI 2006, pp. 231–238 (2006)
12. Garcia-Salicetti, S., Beumier, C., Chollet, G., Dorizzi, B., Jardins, J., Lunter, J., Ni, Y., Petrovska-Delacrétaz, D.: BIOMET: A Multimodal Person Authentication Database Including Face, Voice, Fingerprint, Hand and Signature Modalities. In: Kittler, J., Nixon, M.S. (eds.) AVBPA 2003. LNCS, vol. 2688, pp. 845–853. Springer, Heidelberg (2003)
13. Faraj, M.I., Bigun, J.: Audio-visual person authentication using lip-motion from orientation maps. Pattern Recognition Letters 28(11), 1368–1382 (2007)
14. SHAKE SK6, http://code.google.com/p/shake-drivers

Vibrotactile Recognition by Western and Indian Population Groups of Traditional Musical Scales Played with the Harmonium

Marco Romagnoli[1], Federico Fontana[2], and Ratna Sarkar

[1] University of Verona, Department of Computer Science
strada Le Grazie, 15 – 37134 Verona, Italy
romagnoli@mediasys.it
[2] University of Udine, Department of Mathematics and Computer Science
via delle Scienze, 206 – 33100 Udine, Italy
federico.fontana@uniud.it

Abstract. An experiment was carried out to evaluate the vibrotactile recognition of musical scales produced by an harmonium. The stimuli consisted of four scales played by an Indian performer living in Europe: two western, and two oriental. After listening to the scales without touching the harmonium during a training session, subjects had to put their hands on the instrument and wear headphones emitting a masking noise. Under such conditions they evaluated the same scales, played by the same performer. The experiment was made in Italy and then repeated in India, involving native population groups. Results reveal ability of both groups to recognize the ethnic origin of the scales, limitedly to musicians and with no significant differences between groups. The surprisingly high performance level may suggest possible support during the task of auditory cues capable to bypass the masking noise through bone conduction, and/or perceptual bias due to temporal nuances introduced by the performer. More intriguing appears the hypothesis on possibilities for the musicians to draw from a well-developed tactile memory for tones or harmonic series, result of the training on their acoustic musical instrument. Further experiments would be needed to clarify the importance of touch in the recognition of musical scales, especially for multimodal interface designs in which such temporal patterns may bring significant vibrotactile information to users.

1   Introduction

Research on vibrotactile perception of spatial and temporal patterns is currently receiving recognition, mainly for its increasing importance in multimodal interface design and for informing quality evaluation processes of products with significant non visual interaction components.

With regard to the vibrotactile perception of musical patterns in hearing subjects, studies have been carried out to investigate the importance of vibrotactile feedback for the augmentation or substitution of sonic messages during audio

E.W. Cooper et al. (Eds.): HAID 2011, LNCS 6851, pp. 91–100, 2011.

production/editing operations. To cite one, it has been shown that vibrotactile cues resulting by proper processing of corresponding sounds can be employed for musical instrument labeling, for instance to augment audio mixing consoles [1]. Specifically concerning pitch, experiments making use of vocal stimuli possessing a definite intonation have demonstrated that vibrotactile frequencies can be associated to correct auditory pitch values by subjects without training [2].

In the context of the current psychological and applied research trend toward a more systematic inclusion of vibrotactile devices in musical interfaces [3,4,5], the proposed study investigates the subjective discrimination of musical scales based on touch. Compared to previous experiments [1] in which temporal patterns were fundamental to characterize the tactile stimulus, core in this study is the subjective ability to associate vibrotactile frequencies to pitch [2]. As opposed to studies in which the multimodal integration of joint audio-tactile harmonics was object of investigation, in particular concerning the subjective ability to match tactile frequency components to auditory tones in different multimodal setups [6,7], during our experimental task purely vibrotactile stimuli were provided in form of musical scales after a training session, in which subjects had to listen to the same scales with no exposition to vibrotactile feedback.

1.1 Design Applications

Assessing the salience of the tactile modality in the perception of musical notes is in principle important when designing virtual acoustic musical instruments such as digital pianos [8], electronic drum pads, and similar products currently marketed by the industry also in the form of real time sound synthesis software running on diverse types of computing platforms.

Concerning the more general application field of interaction design, the vibrotactile perception of musical scales has potential to enable peripheral communication in diverse interfaces, especially on wearable devices, where this feedback may be conveyed to implicitly steer one's attention before providing more explicit (say, visual and/or auditory) contextual messaging.

2 Musical Scales with the Harmonium

Most psychophysical research in music perception refers to the Western tradition. Cross-cultural studies considering the perception of musical scales are less common [9]. In general, scales and intervals strongly vary among cultures worldwide. Similarly, the numbers of notes and spaces in-between differ depending on the ethnic origin of a scale. The tonal relations between notes, like the octave, are instead universal.

The harmonium, see Fig. 1, is a free reed aerophone patented in Paris by Debain in 1848. It is played by pressing note keys, while providing air at the desired pressure through the movement of the bellows behind the keyboard. The British introduced the harmonium in India during the colonial period, and then the instrument was quickly adopted in the local culture of that country.

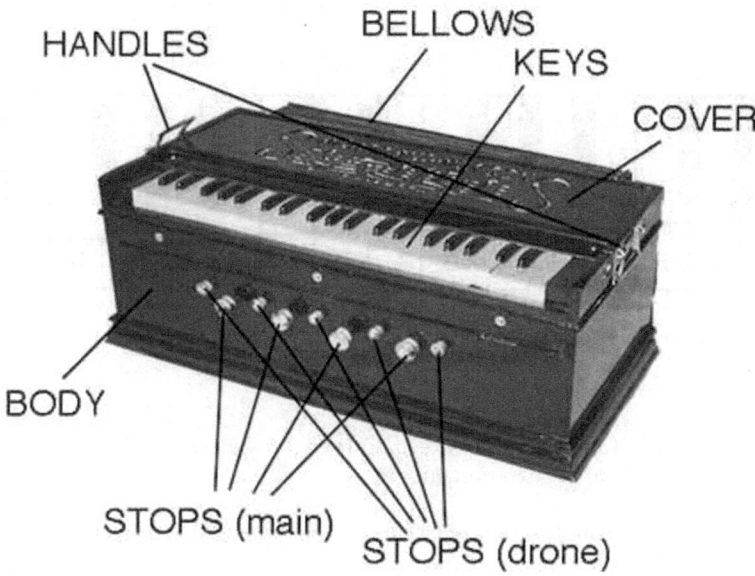

Fig. 1. Harmonium

For its birth in Europe and use mainly in India, it represents a case of musical instrument spanning different cultures.

Fig. 2 shows the harmonium keyboard. The numbers appearing in correspondence to the keys starting from the note A_3 represent vibrotactile fundamental frequencies of the notes used during the experiment, computed for those keys by attaching a measurement accelerometer at the center of the instrument cover and then figuring out the spectrum of the resulting signals.

One spectrum of the acceleration signal for the note D_4 is shown in Fig. 3, as an example of these measurements. At about 150 Hz a component is found, whose frequency amounts to half the fundamental measured value of 295 Hz. This specific partial, located half way the fundamental frequency, was found on all measured acceleration signals, furthermore it was present also in acoustic measurement checks of the same notes made using a microphone. Its generation appears to be specific to the mechanical sound production mechanism of the harmonium.

In Table 1 a comparison is provided between fundamental frequency-equivalent Indian and Western notes. In the Western octave $C\ D\ E\ F\ G\ A\ B\ C$, the C note (corresponding to the Indian *Rsava* in the Indian scales used in this experiment) is repeated at the end of the scale. This repetition does not take place in the Indian tradition, whose musical scale is called *Surasaptaka*, meaning the combination of seven notes [10]. Furthermore some Indian notes are played with more freedom than in the Western tradition, in such a way that a wider range of tonalities can fall in the same note.

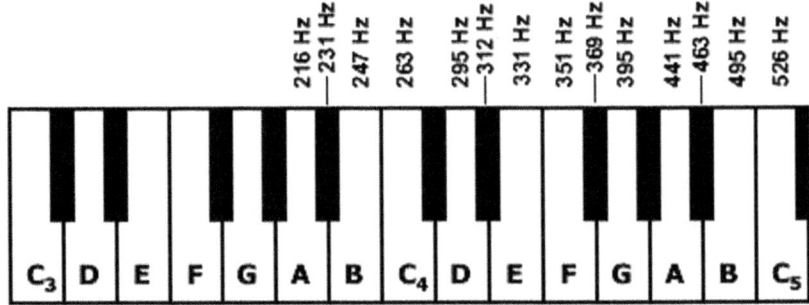

Fig. 2. Harmonium keyboard and associated vibrotactile fundamentals used during the tests

Table 1. Indian note (name and symbol) and their Western equivalents in the case of the Indian scales used in the experiment

Indian note (name)	Indian note (abbv.)	Indian symbol	Western note
Sadaja	Sa	S	$A_{\sharp 3}$ or B_{b3}
Rsava	Re	R	C_4
Gandhara	Ga	G	D_4
Madhyama	Ma	M	$D_{\sharp 4}$ or E_{b4}
Paincama	Pa	P	F_4
Daevata	Da	D	G_4
Nisada	Ni	N	A_4

In consequence of the dependency of musical listening on the traditional scale, people listen to the notes depending on their cultural background. For our research, it is interesting to know that when Indian and Western musicians must evaluate intervals between the notes, their estimates vary depending on whether the listened notes respectively belong to an Indian or Western scale [9]. More in general, the recognition of the ethnic origin of musical scales occurs quite naturally in musicians or in subjects who have a normal understanding of music.

3   Experiment

Two groups of five subjects based respectively in Italy and India, including two teachers of music and three practitioners, had to choose the ethnic origin of four scales by relying on vibrotactile perception through the hands of the vibrations coming from an harmonium manufactured by Orient. By making use of the setup in Fig. 4, which included a pair of Senheiser in-ear headphones, subjects were protected from visual and auditory cues. In parallel they could impose their hands on the upper back side of the instrument, in correspondence of the cover on top of the hammers.

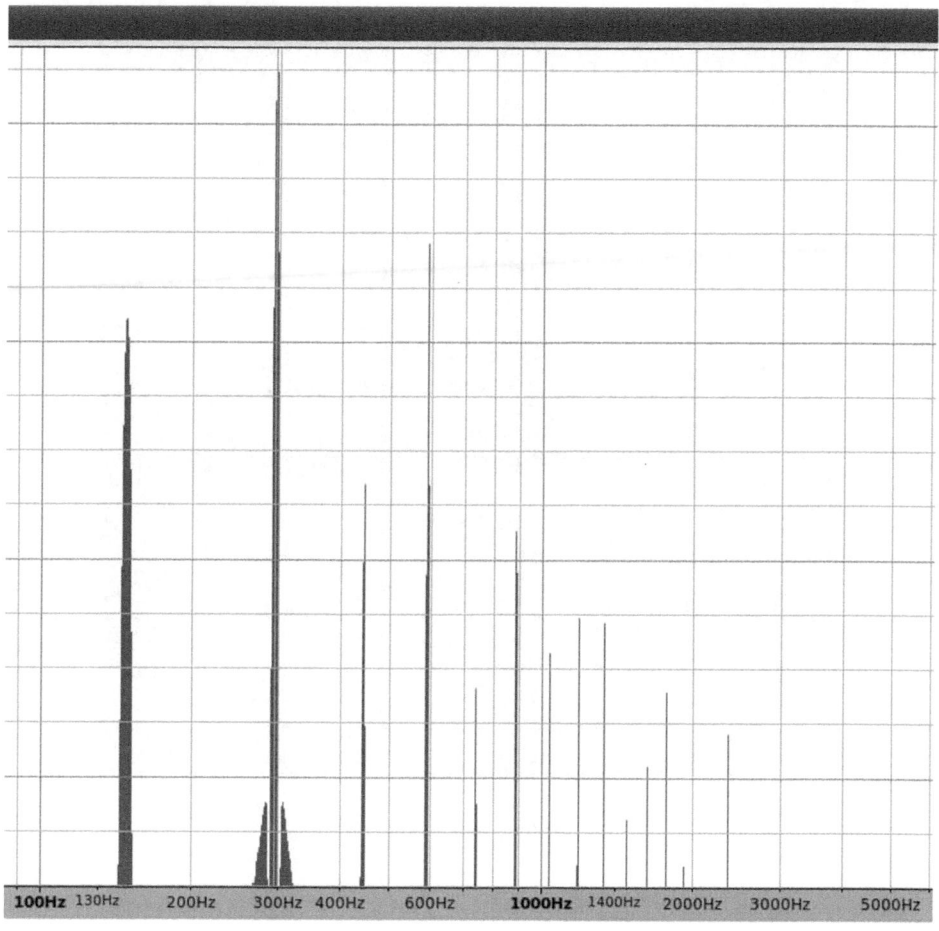

100Hz 130Hz   200Hz   300Hz 400Hz   600Hz   1000Hz 1400Hz 2000Hz 3000Hz   5000Hz

Fig. 3. Acceleration spectrum of the note D_4

Two Western and two Indian scales were selected as stimuli for the experiment:

- C natural (C_4 D_4 E_4 F_4 G_4 A_4 B_4 C_5) and A minor (A_3 B_3 C_4 D_4 E_4 F_4 G_4 A_4) formed two (i.e., the Western) stimuli;
- *Raag Bhairav* (S r G M P d N S) and *Raag Yaman-Kalyan* (S R G m P D N S) formed two (i.e., the Indian) stimuli[1].

As opposed to chords or melodies, musical scales have been selected as stimuli for this experiment because of their relative neutrality with respect to possible spatial localization of the vibrotactile patterns (especially the transients

---

[1] Half tones are denoted using lower-case symbols according to the Indian notation. In particular, the correspondence between Indian and Western notes yields the following equivalents for the Indian half-tones of interest in the experiment: $r = B$, $m = E$, and $d = F_\sharp$ or G_b.

Fig. 4. Setup

elicited by the hammers) or intelligibility of recurrent temporal patterns, respectively. For this reason, all four scales shared the same spatial extension in the harmonium keyboard furthermore having similar intervals between their notes. Moreover, in order to minimize temporal and intensity cues otherwise providing information about the specific scale, the performer took particular care in ensuring an as most invariant tempo, duration, and dynamics during playing[2], meanwhile pumping air into the instrument only prior to the execution of every scale to avoid interfering vibrations due to the mechanics of the bellows.

Before the task, every subject could observe the setup. Then, she was asked to sit down and listen to the four scales for 3-4 minutes, without touching the harmonium. Once in condition to recognize all scales with no effort by listening, every subject had to wear the headphones, through which pink noise was displayed. Finally, again without touching the harmonium, every subject negotiated with the experimenter the noise level at which the instrument, played at maximum volume, could not be heard.

---

[2] A more robust experimental setup should have included an harmonium controller consisting of a robotic arm or similar mechanical device.

Table 2. Individual subjective performance

Subject typology	Western subject		Indian subject	
	Recognition of tradition	Recognition of scale	Recognition of tradition	Recognition of scale
A - teacher of music	7/16	4/16	12/16	12/16
B - teacher of music	11/16	9/16	13/16	11/16
C - amateur musician	15/16	12/16	13/16	8/16
D - professional musician	16/16	12/16	10/16	7/16
E - professional musician	13/16	11/16	10/16	5/16
Overall recognition	62/80	48/80	58/80	43/80
Overall percentage	77.5%	60%	72.5%	53.75%
Random percentage	50%	25%	50%	25%

During the task subjects kept their hands in contact with the harmonium, while the performer repeatedly played one of the four scales. As soon as a scale was guessed, the subject stopped the performer by raising her hands. Then, a choice was made along with a confidence rate. Every scale was repeated four times, for a total of 16 trials keeping subjects busy for about 15 minutes. The experiment was repeated under identical conditions in Italy, in July 2010, and India, in October 2010.

Before the analysis, subjects were selected as to form two samples of five people including two teachers of music and three musicians. All remaining subjects, who had few or no experience in musical teaching or playing, were in fact excluded from both such groups as they were discovered to perform not significantly different from random during a preliminary analysis. The individual performances computed from the selected samples are listed in Table 2, for both Western and Indian listeners.

Finally, it must be reported that all subjects were disturbed during the test by the masking noise. Even if all of them had negotiated its loudness prior to the task as explained above, a few subjects abandoned the experiment lamenting excessive noise level coming from the earphones. Obviously, these subjects were excluded from the analysis. Nor we were able to set up alternatives making possible the masking of the auditory feedback, since solutions such as ear plugs with additional loudspeaker noise proved to be insufficient to mask the sound coming from the harmonium.

4   Results

Single population proportion tests state that both groups correctly classify the origin of the scales (p-values equal to $3.86 \cdot 10^{-9}$ and $6.57 \cdot 10^{-6}$, respectively for the Western and Indian population groups assuming a 50% random choice of the scale origin), as well as the scales themselves (p-values equal to $1.66 \cdot 10^{-10}$ and $2.50 \cdot 10^{-7}$, respectively for the Western and Indian population groups assuming a 25% random choice of the scale).

Furthermore, the two groups do not perform significantly different: a two binomial population proportions test states that there is not sufficient evidence in favor of a difference in the percentages of listeners, judging both the scales (p-value equal to 0.21) and their ethnic origin (p-value equal to 0.23) [11].

Four out of five subjects belonging to the Western group rated their choices with high confidence (i.e., average rates between 4 and 5), whereas one gave a low rating. In India, one subject concluded the test meanwhile being unable to give a confidence rating due to the masking noise, that was judged to be excessively loud.

5   Discussion

The confirmation of the hypothesis poses a number of questions that should need to be further investigated, and whose answer is by all means beyond the scope and technical possibilities of the proposed experiment.

The first question is whether the experimental setup prevented from *any* form of transmission of auditory cues to the subjects. At current it is impossible to attempt even a qualitative answer to this question. Bone conduction, in fact, is a known phenomenon involving the transmission of mechanical waves from the skin to the auditory nerve terminations located in the cochlea. Several contact headphone arrangements exist that exploit this phenomenon. On the other hand, to our knowledge there is no literature devoted to the issue of bone conduction of auditory cues that are delivered in form of vibrations through the hands.

The second question is whether subjects were, even unconsciously, sensitive to intensity or temporal nuances in the performance depending on the specific scale played. Even if they reported to have received no cues of this kind during the experiment while debriefing, this possibility cannot be excluded. One argument that is against this possibility is that any subjective scale discrimination based on vibrotactile intensity or temporal patterns, that had not previously been recorded during the initial acoustic training, should have led subjects to just distinguish one scale from the others without necessarily enabling them to give correct answers. In this situation, a random one-to-one association of such patterns to scales should have brought to an average (i.e., 25%) recognition of the stimuli. As we have seen in Sec. 4 on results, this possibility is contradicted by the experimental results. More in general, doubts on the existence of a perceptual bias due to intensity and/or temporal cues may be cleared either by including a robotic instrument player in the setup, or by implementing some kind of control condition in the experiment itself.

The last issue deals with the low sensitivity of non-musicians to the scales, and their ethnic origin. Since we did not control how many subjects belonging to this group would be able to make a correct choice by merely listening to the four stimuli, it is not obvious to speculate why subjects who could potentially distinguish scales in a conventional listening test were otherwise in trouble in performing the same task when stimulated using vibrations through the hands, as musicians were able to do instead. Provided that musicians were not biased by bone conduction cues and/or patterns depending on the performance — see the above two paragraphs — then it can be hypothesized that these subjects relied on previously encoded ability to discriminate vibrotactile frequencies [12], e.g., a memory for tactile tones that may be especially developed in musicians due to the long training on a musical instrument. In fact, for a given note the fundamental frequency (if not even the first partials of the related harmonic series) produced by most acoustic instruments matches to a good extent with the tones generated by the harmonium in correspondence of the same note. Hence, it may well be that musicians were able to perform a similar matching task at perceptual level based on their tactile memory for frequencies.

In informal support of the existence of this kind of process, it must be reported that some musicians, while debriefing, were confident but at the same time surprised to have reached a high performance in the experiment because, using their own words, during the task they were not in condition to "consciously assess" the vibrotactile feedback as opposed to what happens in a standard listening experiment. These subjective impressions are certainly intriguing, and alone they call for a better understanding of the perceptual as well as brain encoding processes brought to the surface by this experiment.

6   Conclusions

By putting hands on an harmonium on which a performer repeatedly played two western and two oriental musical scales in a random sequence, two independent groups of European and Indian musicians were able to recognize the scales, and hence their ethnic origin, showing significant percentages of success. Such performances were reached after filtering out non-musicians from the samples of populations. This subjective category, in fact, did not show significant percentages of scale recognition.

Motivations explaining this performance can only be hypothesized. In particular, provided that the proposed methodology prevented from transmission of the stimuli through bone conduction, and provided also that subjects were not biased by intensity or temporal patterns involuntarily produced by the performer during playing, then it is possible that musicians relied on a greater ability to discriminate vibrotactile frequencies, encoded in their tactile memory by years of musical instrument training. In this case, further tests involving measurements of brain activity should be set up to gain a better understanding of the outcomes of the proposed experiment, also aiming at the applications envisioned in §1.1.

References

1. Merchel, S., Altinsoy, E., Stamm, M.: Tactile music instrument recognition for audio mixers. In: Proc. 128th AES Convention, London, UK. AES (2010)
2. Rothenberg, M., Molitor, R.D.: Encoding voice fundamental frequency into vibrotactile frequency. J. of the Acoustical Society of America 66, 1029–1038 (1979)
3. Askenfelt, A., Jansson, E.V.: On vibration and finger touch in stringed instrument playing. Music Perception 9, 311–350 (1992)

4. Galembo, A., Askenfelt, A.: Quality assessment of musical instruments - effects of multimodality. In: 5th Triennial Conference of the European Society for the Cognitive Sciences of Music (ESCOM 5), Hannover, Germany (2003)
5. Miranda, E.R., Wanderley, M.M.: New Digital Musical Instruments: Control and Interaction Beyond the Keyboard. A-R Editions, Middleton (2006)
6. Altinsoy, E.: Auditory-Tactile interaction in Virtual Environments. Shaker Verlag, Aachen (2006), web
   http://www.ias.et.tu-dresden.de/akustik/Mitarbeiter/Altinsoy/data/15.pdf
7. Altinsoy, M., Merchel, S.: Cross-modal frequency matching: Sound and whole-body vibration. In: Nordahl, R., Serafin, S., Fontana, F., Brewster, S. (eds.) HAID 2010. LNCS, vol. 6306, pp. 37–45. Springer, Heidelberg (2010)
8. Guizzo, E.: Keyboard maestro. IEEE Spectrum 47, 32–33 (2010)
9. Wolfe, J.M., Kluender, K.R., Levi, D.M., Bartoshuk, L.M., Herz, R.S., Klatzky, R.L., Lederman, S.J., Merfeld, D.M.: Sensation & Perception, 2nd edn. Sinauer Associates Ltd., Sunderland (2008)
10. Sarkar, S.P.R.: Samgiita: Song, Dance and Instrumental Music. English edn, Ananda Marga, Delhi, India (2007)
11. Illowsky, B., Dean, S.: Collaborative Statistics. Connexions - Rice University, Houston (2008), web http://cnx.org/content/col10522/1.21/
12. Hegner, Y.L., Lee, Y., Grodd, W., Braun, C.: Comparing tactile pattern and vibrotactile frequency discrimination: A human fMRI study. J. Neurophysiology 103, 3115–3122 (2010)

Influence of the Auditory Localization Direction on the Haptic Estimation of Virtual Length

Maik Stamm, M. Ercan Altinsoy, and Sebastian Merchel

Chair of Communication Acoustics, Dresden University of Technology, Germany
Maik.Stamm@tu-dresden.de

Abstract. Haptic feedback can be utilized for solving a variety of different tasks in the virtual world. The identification of virtual shapes and objects is a particularly important task. Stamm et al. strived to detect the basic principles of shape and object identification in virtual worlds while conducting haptic identification experiments with numerous virtual models in a previous study. During the exploration and recognition process subjects experienced various difficulties that directly refer to the basic principles. One of those difficulties is subjects' insufficient spatial orientation in the virtual scene. A promising approach refers to the utilization of auditory localization cues. However, it is important to investigate possible interaction effects of such a multimodal reproduction. This work investigates if the haptic recognition of geometrical characteristics could be influenced by simultaneously reproduced localization cues. Specifically, it is investigated if the auditory localization direction influences the haptic length estimation of virtual objects.

Keywords: haptic virtual objects, length estimation, force-feedback, auditory localization direction, stereophony.

1 Introduction

The haptic sense is of increasing importance in virtual environments because it provides high functionality due to its active and bi-directional nature. It can be utilized for solving a variety of different tasks in the virtual world. One truly important task is the exploration and identification of virtual shapes and objects. In particular, blind users, who cannot study graphical illustrations in books, benefit immensely from making use of their sense of touch. Creating digital models based on graphical illustrations or creating models of real physical items allows them to explore virtual representations, and therefore, to learn more effectively. A similar idea was followed by the PURE-FORM project striving to enable blind users to touch and explore digital models of three-dimensional art forms and sculptures [1]. Providing haptic access to mathematical functions is another exemplary application [2].

Furthermore, the haptic identification of virtual shapes and objects is of great importance for sighted users as well. Studies show that memory performance can be increased significantly using multimodal learning methods [3]. Thus, haptic

E.W. Cooper et al. (Eds.): HAID 2011, LNCS 6851, pp. 101–109, 2011.

identification has great potential in the field of education, e.g., if digitized models or anatomical shapes are explored multimodally instead of solely by being viewed. Another important application refers to medical training or teleoperation in minimally invasive surgery. Due to the poor camera view and the sparsely available visual cues, surgeons have to use their long medical instruments to identify anatomical shapes during surgery (e.g., during the removal of a gallbladder [4]). This is a very challenging task that has to be trained by medical students [5]. Furthermore, utilizing haptic feedback for identifying anatomical shapes is of vital importance for teleoperating surgeons. One last promising application that shall be mentioned refers to the "haptification" of (scientific) data [6][7].

Enabling the user to touch, explore, and finally, to identify such virtual shapes and objects requires a haptic feedback device serving as an interface between the user and the application. This device has to be capable of delivering geometrical cues to the user. However, which basic and perceptually relevant information has to be delivered at least to explore and identify virtual shapes and objects effectively and successfully? Stamm et al. strived to detect these basic principles. Therefore, identification experiments with geometric primitives as well as modifications of them have been conducted in a previous study [8], whereby the participant's exploratory procedure was constrained as much as possible [9]. Due to this limitation they could only perceive a reduced set of information, thus experiencing various difficulties during the exploration and recognition process (e.g., in detecting edges and corners, in discriminating similar curvature or slope and in locating current exploration position) [8]. These difficulties refer to the basic principles that have to be addressed scientifically to enable high identification rates in such identification tasks. One of those difficulties is subjects' insufficient spatial orientation in the virtual scene. They often reached the limit of the force-feedback workspace unconsciously and assumed that there was an object. Another problem occurred if the subjects explored the surface of a virtual object and approached towards an edge or a corner at one of its sides. Normally, the haptic interaction point (HIP) slipped off the object and got lost in the virtual space. That is why subjects lost orientation and they could not locate the HIP in relation to the object. They needed a lot of time to get in contact with it again and usually had to continue the exploration process at a completely different position on the surface. This considerable problem was also observed in [10] and makes it quite difficult to explore and identify virtual shapes and objects effectively. Therefore, additional information has to be provided to improve the users' capability of locating the HIP in the virtual space. One promising approach refers to the utilization of auditory localization cues that can extend the haptic spatial resolution and increase users' certainty and immersion during the virtual interaction. The usefulness of auditory localization cues for the haptic interaction in virtual spaces was shown in different studies. They were used successfully in haptic-audio navigational tasks, e.g., when users tried to explore, to learn and to manage a route in a virtual traffic environment (ears-in-hand interaction technique, [11]). They were also quite helpful to locate objects in the virtual space [12][13][14]. It is obvious that the virtual haptic shape and object identification will profit too if the current exploration position of the HIP is reproduced with the help of auditory localization cues. However, possible inter-action effects of such a haptic-audio reproduction have to be considered. It would be possible that the haptic recognition of geometrical characteristics could be in-fluenced by simultaneously reproduced localization cues. For instance, the users might misjudge the dimensions of a virtual object. A possibility to investigate the presence of such a distorting influence is described in this work. Specifically, this work investigates if the auditory localization direction influences the haptic length estimation of virtual objects.

2   Spatial Reproduction

A two-channel stereophony setup is used for reproducing the auditory localiza-tion cues. The displacement of the phantom source between the two loudspeakers (base angle $2\phi_0$) at an azimuth angle ϕ to the user is realized by amplitude pan-ning. The gaining factors g_1 and g_2 of the signal $s(t)$ are calculated using the "tangent law" (Figure 1):

$$\frac{\tan\phi}{\tan\phi_0} = \frac{g_1 - g_2}{g_1 + g_2} \tag{1}$$

The "tangent law" is superior to other panning laws in predicting the per-ceived localization direction [15]. To prevent unwanted changes in loudness of the phantom source in dependence of the localization direction, the sum of the squares of the gaining factors has to be normalized:

$$\sqrt{\sum_{n=1}^{2} g_n^2} = g_1^2 + g_2^2 = 1 \tag{2}$$

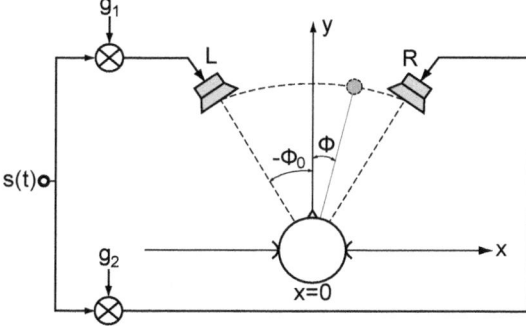

Fig. 1. The displacement of the phantom source between the two loudspeakers (base angle $2\phi_0$) at an azimuth angle ϕ to the user is realized by amplitude panning. The gaining factors g_1 and g_2 of the signal $s(t)$ are calculated using the "tangent law".

3   Experiment

3.1   Setup

The experimental hardware setup is outlined in Figure 2. A computer is used as the control unit. It is connected to a PHANTOM Omni force-feedback device and to a RME Hammerfall DSP Multiface II external sound card. The sound card transmits the weighted acoustic signals to two loudspeakers of the type GENELEC 8040A. To simulate broader acoustic extensions, the aperture of loudspeakers $2\phi_0$ is extended to $90°$ in contrast to classic stereophony setups.

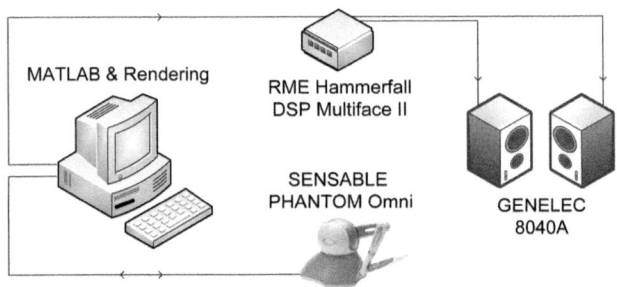

Fig. 2. Experimental hardware setup

The impedance controlled PHANTOM Omni from SensAble Technologies provides 6 degrees-of-freedom (DOF) positional sensing and 3 DOF force-feedback. The small and desk-grounded device consists of a robotic arm with three revolute joints. Each of them is connected to a computer-controlled electric DC motor. When interacting with the device, the user holds a stylus that is attached to the tip of the robot arm. This stylus transmits the calculated forces to the user's hand when the virtual object is being touched. The technical specifications of the PHANTOM Omni haptic device are outlined in [16].

The developed software setup is outlined in Figure 3. MATLAB is used for automating the experimental procedure and for questioning the test subjects with a graphical user interface. MATLAB also initiates the processes for haptic rendering (Chai3D, Stanford University) and acoustic rendering (Pure Data, Open-Source Project). For details on the C++ framework of Chai3D, the algorithms for collision detection, force control and force response, please review [17]. Details on Pure Data are outlined in [18]. To reproduce acoustic signals, Pure Data requires information from the PHANTOM Omni that communicates with Chai3D via a software interface. This information, which relates collisions (whether the user touches the virtual object) and the absolute position of the HIP is steadily transferred to Pure Data via Open Sound Control (OSC). The data are then processed and mapped for subsequent signal output.

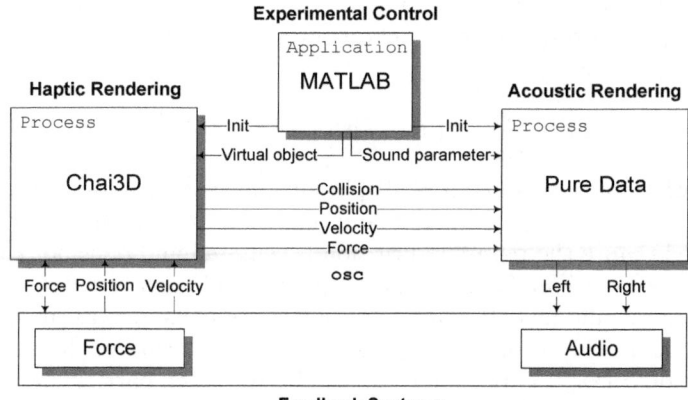

Fig. 3. Experimental software setup

3.2 Stimuli

The test subjects are asked to haptically estimate the length of three virtual cuboids (l_1=6 cm, l_2=7.5 cm and l_3=9 cm). To guarantee identical movement lengths for all participants, the cuboids are cut by a plane frontally (Figure 4). In this way, the exploration movement can be guided along the cut edge in the frontal plane from the left to the right and vice versa (x-axis). The stiffness of the virtual cuboids and the plane is set to 400 N/m.

As soon as the HIP collides with the cuboid and the scanning velocity rises up to $v_{\exp} > 0\frac{\text{cm}}{\text{s}}$, broadband noise is reproduced by the two loudspeakers (L_s=50 dB(A)). The panning direction ϕ is varied according to the current exploration

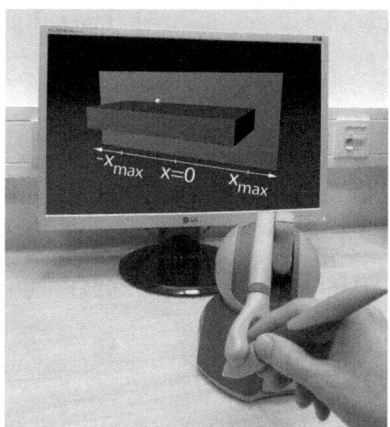

Fig. 4. The virtual cuboids are explored along the cut edge in the frontal plane horizontally (x-axis). The depiction on the screen is rotated slightly for better illustration.

position x. The left border of the cuboid $-x_{max}$ respectively the right border of the cuboid x_{max} corresponds to a maximal displacement of the phantom source at $-\phi_{max}$ respectively $+\phi_{max}$:

$$\phi(x) = \frac{\phi_{max}}{x_{max}} \cdot x \qquad \text{with} \quad x = [-x_{max},\ x_{max}] \qquad (3)$$

Three variations of this maximal displacement are chosen for each of the three cuboids: $|\phi_{max}| = 0°$, $|\phi_{max}| = 22.5°$ and $|\phi_{max}| = 45°$. The first setting is used as reference because the panning direction is centered and does not change with the exploration position. Thus, the participants will hear a broadband noise that is localized in the middle between the two loudspeaker as soon as the HIP collides with the cuboid. The resulting 9 stimuli (cuboid with three different lengths × three variations of ϕ_{max}) are presented two times to each participant to calculate the corresponding mean length estimations. The order of the 18 presentations is randomized.

3.3   Procedure

The test subject is seated on a chair without armrests that is positioned in a distance of 90 centimeters centrally in front of the two loudspeakers (Figure 1). The haptic device is centrally arranged in front of the test subject at a comfortable distance on a table. At the beginning, the subject passes a training session to get used to the device, the exploration process and the estimation of length (with the help of a ruler). Subsequently, the subject is blindfolded and asked to estimate the length of 18 consecutively presented cuboids. The cuboid can be scanned as often as necessary, thus the exploration time is not limited. The subject is instructed that exploration velocity has to be greater than zero centimeters per second to prevent step-wise measuring. Due to this demand, the continuous displacement of the phantom source depending on the current exploration position becomes clearly audible as well. The role of the acoustic signal is not explained or commented. The subjects also get no feedback concerning the accuracy of their estimations.

3.4   Subjects

Fifteen subjects (8 female and 7 male) voluntarily participated in the experiment. Their ages ranged from 20 to 40 years (mean 28 years). Two of them were left-handed. All indicated that they had no hearing damage or hand disorders. They were apprentices, students or employees of Dresden University of Technology and had little to no experience using a haptic force-feedback device.

4   Results and Discussion

The mean values of the estimated lengths are outlined in dependence of the real length of the virtual cuboids as well as in dependence of the maximal displacement ϕ_{max} of the phantom source in Figure 5. Results can be summarized as follows:

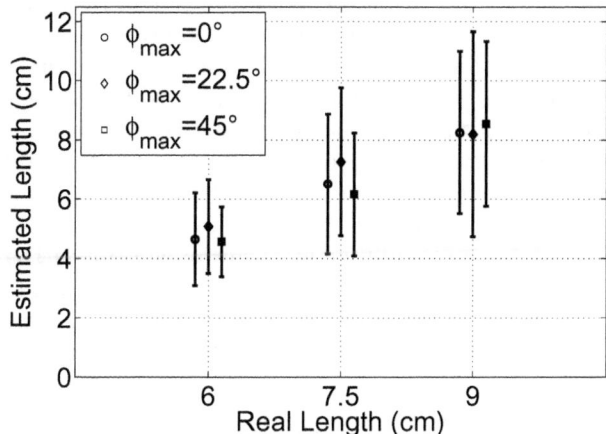

Fig. 5. Mean length estimations ($\pm$ standard deviation) in dependence of the real length of the virtual cuboids as well as in dependence of the maximal displacement ϕ_{max} of the phantom source. Mean values for a specific real length are shifted horizontally for better illustration.

- The subjects underestimate the real lengths of virtual cuboids. The estimations become more accurate for the longer cuboids (mean error in percent: $\overline{\Delta l_1} \approx 20\%$, $\overline{\Delta l_2} \approx 12\%$ and $\overline{\Delta l_3} \approx 8\%$).
- However, the interindividual standard deviations of the mean estimations increase with increasing length.
- The variation of the maximal displacement of the localization direction ($|\phi_{max}| = 22.5°$ and $|\phi_{max}| = 45°$) does not influence the estimation of virtual lengths in comparison to the reference $|\phi_{max}| = 0°$.

It has to be mentioned that it is a complicated task to haptically estimate the length of a virtual object. Although it was not the primary purpose of this study to investigate how accurate subjects can perform such a task, the outlined results confirm the results of [10] concerning the underestimation of real length and concerning the dependence of the mean error on real length. It could be proved that these relations are valid for bigger respectively longer virtual objects as well.

Therefore, if the user is intended to haptically perceive a certain object length, the dimensions of the virtual representation have to be calibrated at first [10]. Another approach refers to the simultaneous addition of appropriate visual information. Because the combination of the haptic and visual modality approach statistical optimality, more accurate estimations can be expected [19].

The purpose of this study was to investigate if the auditory localization direction influences the haptic length estimation of a virtual object and, therefore, if it is possible to easily create a haptic-audio interaction effect that might distort the haptic recognition of the geometrical characteristics of a virtual object. The results demonstrate that the reproduction of stereophonic localization cues does not influence the haptic estimation of horizontally arranged, virtual lengths. There was no distorting haptic-audio interaction effect. Thus, the length perception seems to be dominated by the haptic sense. Nevertheless, subjects' statements indicate that the reproduction of acoustic localization cues is desirable and also helpful for the orientation in the virtual scene. Subjects did not use the cues to estimate the virtual lengths, but rather to locate the HIP in relation to the centrally arranged virtual cuboid. Thus, they combined the scanning movement with the displacement of the phantom source intuitively.

However, the usefulness of auditory localization cues for virtual haptic shape and object identification has to be investigated in future works in detail to take a further considerable step forward in designing highly informative and high-quality audio-haptic feedback systems that can be useful for so many applications.

Acknowledgement. The authors wish to thank Prof. Jekosch for her support and informative discussions as well as the Deutsche Forschungsgemeinschaft (DFG; 156/1-1) for supporting this work.

References

1. Jansson, G., Bergamasco, M., Frisoli, A.: A new option for the visually impaired to experience 3d art at museums: Manual exploration of virtual copies. Visual Impairment Research 5(1), 1–12 (2003)
2. Van Scoy, F.L., Kawai, T., Darrah, M., Rash, C.: Haptic display of mathematical functions for teaching mathematics to students with vision disabilities: Design and proof of concept. In: Brewster, S., Murray-Smith, R. (eds.) Haptic HCI 2000. LNCS, vol. 2058, pp. 31–40. Springer, Heidelberg (2001)
3. Sepulveda-Cervantes, G., Parra-Vega, V., Dominguez-Ramirez, O.: Haptic cues for effective learning in 3d maze navigation. In: IEEE International Workshop on Haptic Audio visual Environments and Games, HAVE 2008, pp. 93–98 (2008)
4. Keehner, M., Lowe, R.K.: Seeing with the hands and with the eyes: The contributions of haptic cues to anatomical shape recognition in surgery. Association for the Advancement of Artificial Intelligence (2009)
5. Holland, K.L., Williams II, R.L., Conatser Jr., R.R., Howell, J.N., Cade, D.L.: The implementation and evaluation of a virtual haptic back. Virtual Reality Society 7, 94–102 (2004)
6. Faeth, A., Oren, M., Harding, C.: Combining 3-d geovisualization with force feedback driven user interaction. In: ACM SIGSPATIAL International Conference on Advances in Geographic Information Systems, Irvine, CA, USA (2008)
7. Qi, W.: Geometry based haptic interaction with scientific data. In: ACM International conference on Virtual reality continuum and its applications, Hong Kong (2006)
8. Stamm, M., Altinsoy, M.E., Merchel, S.: Identification Accuracy and Efficiency of Haptic Virtual Objects Using Force-Feedback. In: 3rd International Workshop on Perceptual Quality of Systems, Bautzen, Germany (2010)
9. Lederman, S.J., Klatzky, R.L.: Haptic identification of common objects: Effects of constraining the manual exploration process. Perception & Psychophysics 66, 618–628 (2004)

10. Colwell, C., Petrie, H., Kornbrot, D.: Use of a haptic device by blind and sighted people: Perception of virtual textures and objects. In: Placencia, I., Porrero, E. (eds.) Improving the Quality of Life for the European Citizen: Technology for Inclusive Design and Equality. IOS Press, Amsterdam (1998)
11. Magnusson, C., Rassmus-Grohn, K.: A virtual traffic environment for people with visual impairment. Visual Impairment Research 7(1), 1–12 (2005)
12. Magnusson, C., Rassmus-Grhn, K.: Audio haptic tools for navigation in non visual environments. In: The 2nd International Conference on Enactive Interfaces, ENACTIVE 2005, Genoa, Italy, pp. 17–18 (2005)
13. Murphy, E., Moussette, C., Verron, C., Guastavino, C.: Design and evaluation of an audio-haptic interface. In: eNTERFACE, Orsay-Paris, France (2008)
14. Wood, J., Magennis, M., Francisca, E., Arias, C., Gutierrez, T., Bergamasco, M.: The design and evaluation of a computer game for the blind in the grab haptic audio virtual environment. In: EuroHaptics (2003)
15. Pulkki, V.: Spatial Sound Generation and Perception by Amplitude Panning Techniques. Ph.D. thesis, Helsinki University of Technology (2001)
16. SensAble Technologies: PHANTOM OMNI Technical Specifications (2010), http://www.sensable.com
17. Conti, F., Barbagli, F., Morris, D., Sewell, C.: Chai 3D - Documentation (2009), http://www.chai3d.org
18. Open Source Project: Pure Data - Documentation (2011), http://puredata.info/
19. Gepshtein, S., Banks, M.S.: Viewing geometry determines how vision and haptics combine in size perception. Current Biology 13, 483–488 (2003)

Auditory Brain-Computer/Machine-Interface Paradigms Design

Tomasz M. Rutkowski[1,2]

[1] Life Science Center of TARA, University of Tsukuba, Tsukuba, Ibaraki, Japan
[2] RIKEN Brain Science Institute, Wako-shi, Saitama, Japan
tomek@tara.tsukuba.ac.jp
http://www.tara.tsukuba.ac.jp/~tomek/

Abstract. The paper discusses novel and interesting, from users' point of view, design of auditory brain-computer/machine interfaces (BCI/ BMI) utilizing human auditory responses. Two concepts of auditory stimuli BCI/BMI are presented. The first paradigm is based on steady-state tonal or musical stimuli yielding satisfactory EEG response classification for several seconds long stimuli. The second discussed paradigm is based on spatial sound localization and the brain evoked responses estimation, requiring shorter than a second stimuli presentation. In conclusion the preliminary results are discussed and suggestions for further applications are drawn.

Keywords: brain-computer-interface, brain-machine-interface, auditory neuroscience.

1 Introduction

Brain computer and brain machine interfaces (BCI/BMI) [4] are the emerging human-machine interaction technologies that require only user's intentional brain activity modulation to generate commands. At the center of such interactive neurotechnolgy applications are adaptive machine learning applications and carefully designed BCI/BMI paradigms that allow for a capture and further classification of human brain activity patterns later translated to the interfacing commands. BCI/BMI do not require any behavioral activities usually utilized in classical human-computer/machine-interfacing (HCI/HMI). The monitored and adaptively classified brain activity patterns (usually preceding any behavior) are only necessary. This allows for creating a perfect interactive interfacing technology for paralyzed or locked-in patients who cannot execute any bodily movements or peripheral nervous system perceptions. The healthy users also benefit from the BCI/BMI in computer gaming, smart environments control or bodily training/rehabilitation technologies. The majority of contemporary BCI/BMI applications relay on movement imagery [20] or visual stimuli paradigms [5] which are known for their very heavy attentional resources requirements. The auditory and somatosensory (especially haptic) sensory modalities are not yet fully explored. Two auditory BCI/BMI paradigm candidates are discussed in

E.W. Cooper et al. (Eds.): HAID 2011, LNCS 6851, pp. 110–119, 2011.

this paper which result with very promising classification accuracies. Auditory BCI/BMI neurotechnology applications or generally research on brain responses to audio stimuli are usually based on the monitoring of brain electrical activity by means of the electroencephalogram (EEG) [8]. Owing to its non-invasive nature, the EEG based BCI/BMI are the best candidates to be at the core of future "intelligent" interfacings applications and prosthetic devices. A concept of utilizing brain auditory modality creates a very interesting possibility to target "a less crucial" auditory sensory domain, which is not as demanding as vision during operation of machinery or visual computer applications. Auditory BCI/BMI is thus potentially a less mentally demanding paradigm receiving recently more attention in computational neuroscience applications [13,15,17]. We propose to utilize both tonal and spatial audio stimuli cues based designs with a target application in a new BCI/BMI paradigms where users intentionally direct their attention to different sounds or their locations in surround sound environment. In order to identify user's target responses to presented tonal or spatial stimuli we first have to preprocess the EEG signals in order to decompose them into components carrying stimuli evoked potentials (so called auditory-steady-state-responses or event-related potentials). In order to achieve this we utilize a signal processing pipeline composed of EMD technique with spectral clustering followed by signals averaging and their locations estimation which is not discussed in this paper (refer to [14]).

In the following sections we review two auditory BCI/BMI techniques based on tonal/musical monaural stimuli and later on spatial cues identification. Obtained results discussion concludes the paper.

2 Auditory Steady-State Response (ASSR) and Musical Stimuli Brain Interfacing Paradigms

Tonal (ASSR) and musical stimuli belong to common ambient auditory environment components thus they sound usually very natural to humans. We propose to utilize such common sounds as interfacing commands carriers to which users direct their attention or ignore them. The estimated brain responses confirming attentional choices are further estimated in order translated them to commands. The ASSR response itself is an evoked neural potential that follows the envelope of a complex auditory stimulus. It is evoked by a periodic modulation, or turning ON/OFF of a tone or an auditory flutter [1]. The neural response to the ASSR stimulus follows closely the envelope modulation signal; this makes it perfectly suited for basic study of auditory responses. This is clear due to the fact that ASSR is longer and conveys more user–friendly information as comparing to short clicks and beeps used in standard auditory evoked potential (AEP) studies [9,11]. Steady–state brain electrical responses to auditory stimuli can be recorded over a range of AM and FM modulation rates. It has been also shown that different modulation results in stimulation of different areas of the auditory pathway in the brain sites [1]. In the [18] it was shown that lower frequency stimuli rates ($f_m < 20$Hz) cause activity of the generators responsible for late-latency responses, moderate rates ($f_m = 20$Hz,..., 60Hz) are responsible for the middle-latency response, and higher rates ($f_m > 60$Hz) reflect activity from the brainstem. For experiments reported in this paper a frequency set of $f_m \in \{7, 10, 13, 17, 21, 27, 31\}$Hz was chosen to cover lower frequency ranges which are more dependent on subject's state and motivational/attentional control[1] and the middle range frequencies, which are less affected by subject's mental states.

ASSR Experiments and Results. In all the experiments, human subjects are listening to auditory stimuli of different types: AM modulated tones, music, and background noise (pre-STIM). The latter is produced by the air-conditioning and electronic equipment in the EEG laboratory. The musical stimulus is the well-known overture of Beethoven's Symphony No. 5. The subjects had heard this musical piece before. The ASSR tonal patterns are chosen to evoke oscillatory brain activity at the same frequencies as amplitude modulating frequency within the stimuli as the tone modulation. Two tones with carrier frequencies $f_m \in \{500, 1500\}$Hz are chosen since they are located within "the best hearing area" for an average human subject [18]. Both tones are further amplitude modulated with $f_m \in \{7, 10, 13, 17, 21, 27, 31\}$Hz and duration of 300ms for each segment, thus composing 2100ms long tonal chirps. The subjects are stimulated in segments of the order: 5s of no stimuli; 5s break; 5s ASSR 500Hz chirp (the middle part of 2s taken later for analysis); 5s break; 5s ASSR 1500Hz chirp (the middle part of 2s taken later for analysis); 5s break; 5s of music (the middle part of 2s taken later for analysis). This sequence is repeated 12 times for each subject.

For all experiments the EEG signals are recorded using g.USBamps^{TM} system by g.tec[2], from 12 locations (four frontal: $Fp1, Fp2, F3, F4$; six auditory cortex areas: $C3, C5, T7, C4, C6, T8$; two parietal $P3, P4$) [8]. To that end an advanced EEG analysis approach as in [14] is utilized.

Subjects are asked, during all experiments, to concentrate on reading text presented on a computer display. The information to which stimuli to attend is also shown before each stimulus (top-down/anticipation modeling).

All experiments are conducted in the Advanced Brain Signal Processing Laboratory, RIKEN Brain Science Institute in Saitama, Japan with agreement of the institute's ethical guidelines. The sounds are played through stereophonic loudspeakers located in a "noisy" laboratory (computer workstations, air-conditioner, ventilation, etc.) in order to generate so called "environmental noise".

EEG Intradependence Analysis Methods for ASSR. At the EEG feature extraction stage we consider intradependence techniques [3,12], in order to find features which will be later used for classification of different attentional brain stages resulting from presented auditory stimuli. The intradependence measures

---

[1] To follow a paradigm that *attention can be modeled as a top-down mechanism of modulation perception*

[2] The EEG recording system details are accessible at http://www.gtec.at/

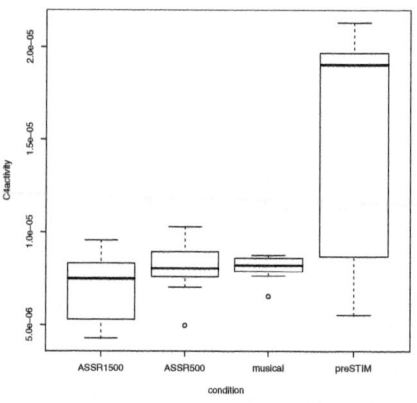

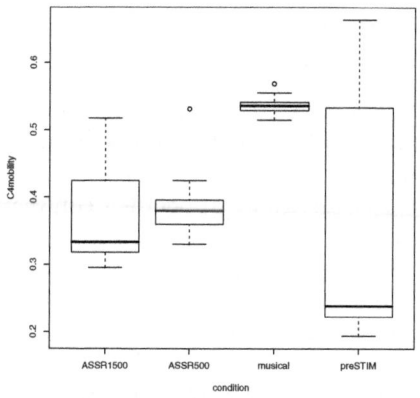

(a) Hjorth activity at the electrode $C4$. (significance $p < 0.001$).

(b) Hjorth mobility at the electrode $C4$ (significance $p < 0.001$).

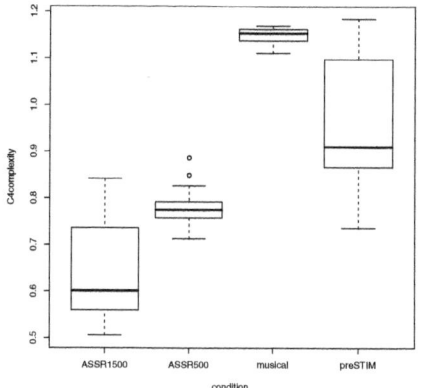

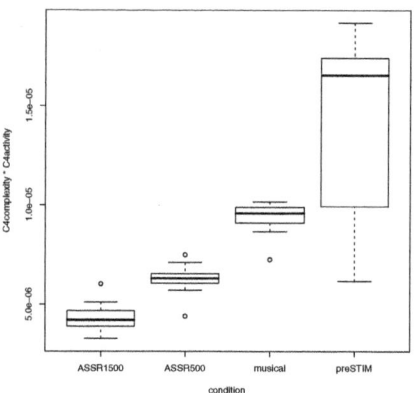

(c) Hjorth complexity at the electrode $C4$ (significance level $p < 0.001$).

(d) Hjorth activity and complexity components combined at the electrode $C4$ (lowering even more significance $p \lll 0.001$).

Fig. 1. KW and the TukeyHSD test analyses results for $C4$ electrode and Hjorth components

considered in this paper are Hjorth [6,16] activity, mobility and complexity components discussed below.

The three Hjorth's components are based on time domain analysis and are defined as

Activity: computed as a variance of short-time EEG signal segments;

Mobility: computed as the square root of the activity of the first derivative of
the signal to the activity of the analyzed EEG;

Complexity: defined as a ratio of the mobility of the first derivative of EEG
to the mobility itself.

Analysis of 2s EEG segments recorded from the subjects with 12 auditory trials
each with utilization of components proposed by [6] shows the possibility for further discrimination among particular stimuli groups, thus allowing for BCI/BMI
interface design by appending commands to attentional choices of the stimuli by
the users.

After a preliminary analysis of Hjorth components distributions and their
differences of mean values for different classes four electrodes were chosen for
detailed statistical analysis. These were $C3,F3,Fp1,P3$, for the following reasons: (i) more pronounced differences for different pairs of stimuli; (ii) known
reports from literature about attentional EEG modulations recorded from those
sites [8]. Since the assumptions of the analysis of variance (ANOVA) test may not
always be met, we decided to use Post-hoc Tukey Honest Significance Difference
(Tukey HSD) to show the possibility of discriminating the responses based on
2s EEG segments analysis of means [10]. These results (Tukey HSD for Hjorth
components of the set of $\{C3, F3, Fp1, P3\}$ electrodes) prompted a possibility
to create simple classification engines capable of discrimination among tonal and
musical brain responses. Table 1 shows results of classification when SVMs (with
two parameters only to avoid overfilling) classifiers [2] were applied to classify
all the three values of Hjorth components.

Analysis of two seconds of EEG segments recorded during 24 auditory sessions for each subject with utilization of components proposed by [6] shows very
interesting results allowing simple discrimination of particular stimuli groups as
shown in Figure 1.

Table 1. Percentage of incorrectly classified tonal & musical BCI/BMI responses using Hjorth activity, mobility and complexity components with SVM classifiers [2] and
leave–one–out cross–validation

Hjorth component	Classifier type	Estimated error
Activity	SVM{*linear*}	31%
	SVM{*radial*}	30%
Mobility	SVM{*linear*}	40%
	SVM{*radial*}	34%
Complexity	SVM{*linear*}	21%
	SVM{*radial*}	22%

2.1   Auditory Evoked Responses Based Spatial BCI/BMI Paradigms

A concept of a spatial auditory stimulus creates a very interesting possibility to
target "the less crucial" auditory activity. We propose to utilize spatial audio
stimuli design with a target application in a new BCI/BMI paradigms where

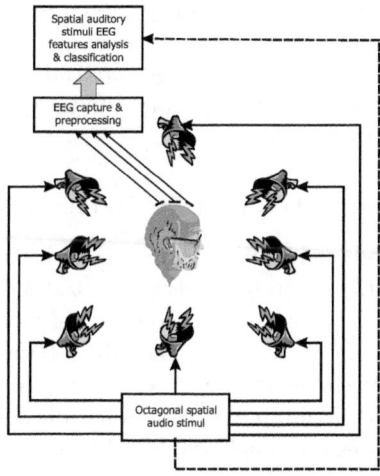

Fig. 2. Spatial auditory BCI/BMI paradigm concept

users concoiusly direct their attention to different locations in surround sound environment with various tonal frequency stimuli [13] as depicted in Figure 2. Contemporary applications limit their scope to frontal surround sound loudspeakers [17], while our proposal includes also rear loudspeakers sound presentation allowing for eight commands BCI/BMI applications (octagonal loudspeakers setup).

In the approach first proposed in [15] it was shown that responses in a spatial tonal stimuli within the 7.1 channels surround sound system (subjects were positioned in the middle of the loudspeakers systems and requested to direct attention to single direction loudspeakers) were distinguishable in EEG for targets and non-targets interfacing commands. The target and non-target direction sequences were presented randomly in the 1/7 ratio. The current proposal extends the design to fully octagonal loudspeakers setup with stimuli sequences presented randomly in the 1/8 ratio.

Within this framework, the subjects are asked to focus their attention to a direction of the tonal or environmental sound. The EEG responses are recorded with the EEG amplifier. Additionally vertical and horizontal eye-movements are recorded in order to have a reference signal indicting potential muscle activity used later in artifacts removal algorithm. We utilize previously proposed by the authors approach utilizing empirical mode decomposition (EMD) technique combined with frequency domain clustering scheme as in [14]. This way, the multichannel and multimodal signal decomposition technique uses the EEG captured by several electrodes located over auditory and temporal brain areas, subsequently preprocessed, and transformed into informative time-frequency traces, which very accurately visualize frequency and amplitude with utilization of a multichannel extension of the univariate EMD [7,14]. This approach allows us to separate from all EEG channels only the components carrying brain activities with stimuli depended components to which subjects attend in spatial environment. The so obtained brain activity spatial patterns clearly follow the expectations of stronger activities in auditory and temporal cortical areas related to the attended sound directions.

2.2   Spatial Auditory BCI/BMI Interfacing Design Results

Finally the reconstructed neurophysiological signals are averaged to compare target and non-target evoked potentials as visualized in Figure 3. The result presented in Table 2 show that it is possible to discriminate brain evoked responses with highest differences in 265ms area (so called P300 or "*aha*" response) to target (expected) spatial sound locations and the ignored ones. Such very fast brain responses to spatial stimuli presentations allow for interactive auditory interfacing applications design which would allow for "hands-free" operation of multi-command (eight commands in presented proposal) interfaces. As an example of the target application driving of a wheelchair (each of eight commands relating to an intended movement direction as in virtual auditory space reproduced via headphones: front, back, left, right, etc.) or virtual computer mouse (similar movement of a cursor on a computer display management) for paralyzed or "locked-in" people.

Table 2. Percentage of incorrectly classified spatial audio BCI/BMI P300 ("*aha*") responses with SVM classifiers [2] and leave–one–out cross–validation

EEG feature	Classifier type	Estimated error
P300 area	SVM{*linear*}	18%
	SVM{*radial*}	11%

3   Discussion

Two auditory BCI/BMI paradigms based on tonal and spatial cues have been discussed in the paper. We have observed a very interesting possibility to classify brain EEG responses during ASSR and musical stimulation which have been found as potentially very promising for "musical/auditory BMI/BCI". The proposed three classes of auditory stimuli have been analyzed extensively with intradependency measures revealing very interesting patterns and possibility to estimate brain attention states as a function of presented auditory stimuli. This is a step forward for auditory-selective-attention evaluation based on top-down neural anticipatory processes estimation.

The evaluated intradependency measures in form of Hjorth coefficients extracted from 2s segments of single channel EMD preprocessed EEG signals have been further classified. The results are very encouraging for both statistical analysis and SVM classification trials. The only drawback have been identified the 2 seconds long segments which could cause delays in BCI/BMI designs.

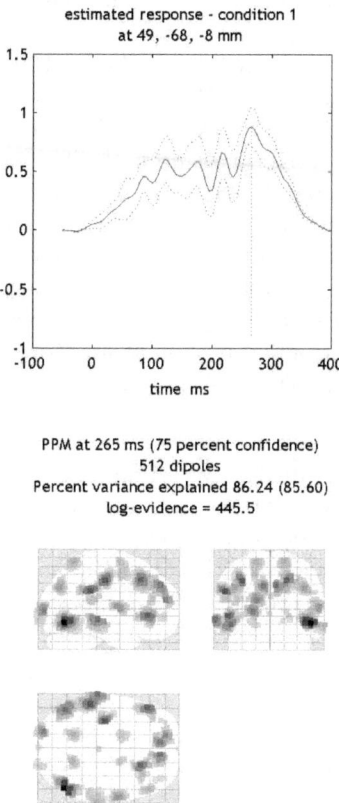

Fig. 3. The results of EEG contrasts for target and non-target (the upper panel of the above figure) mapping at 265ms after stimulus onset in response to spatial audio stimuli showing possibility to discriminate spatial activity maps based on the user's attention. These results show that around 265ms after stimuli onset subject's brain reacts differently and this could be already captured by EEG. The lower panel of the figure presents the estimated sources of the elucidated ERP as visualized with SPM8 [19].

The presented study is highly relevant for brain computer/machine interfaces (BCI/BMI) and the obtained results show that ASSR and mostly musical stimuli based BCI/BMI have a very high potential for future applications; moreover, such systems can be used by most subjects without prior training. However, state-of-the-art ASSR and musical stimuli based BCI/BMI systems require very heavy signal processing and response detection techniques, and therefore, they yield relatively low data rates. This is largely due to the fact that those systems typically only use the power spectrum as input features, in particular, the power spectrum at the ASSR and musical stimulation frequencies. As our study shows, EEG modality have strong potential for ASSR detection despite the short stimulation period (only 2 to 5s), we obtained low classification errors (below 21% at best).

We also presented a proposal to create the spatial sound directed attention paradigm as a candidate for BCI/BMI technologies which in comparison to contemporary application utilizes also the rear direction (behind the head) loudspeakers to introduce more possible commands. This has allowed for implementation of a fully "eight-commands" BCI/BMI paradigm leading to nearly perfect classification results with very fast responses of 265ms after stimuli presentation.

This is a step forward in auditory modality based interfacing design which could be useful primarily for creating novel and user friendly brain-machine-interfaces that would be flexible, adaptive and response automatic based on the detection of subject's intentional direction to auditory content or spatial focused attention, thus resulting in fast estimation of user's intention in relation to the presented spatial stimuli.

Acknowledgments. The author would like to thank Sungyoung Kim and Masahiro Ikeda of YAMAHA Corporation for their technical support and rental of an experimental spatial auditory equipment used for the experiments. This research was supported in part by KAKENHI, the Japan Society for the Promotion of Science grant no. 21360179 and in part by Royal Society International Joint Project grants.

References

1. Bendor, D., Wang, X.: Differential neural coding of acoustic flutter within primate auditory cortex. Nature Neuroscience 10, 763–771 (2007)
2. Chang, C.C., Lin, C.J.: Libsvm: a library for support vector machines (2007)
3. Chen, M., Rutkowski, T.M., Jelfs, B., Souretis, G., Cao, J., Mandic, D.: Assessment of nonlinearity in brain electrical activity: A DVV approach. In: Proceedings of The 2007 RISP International Workshop on Nonlinear Circuits and Signal Processing, March 3-7, pp. 461–464. Shanghai Jiao Tong University, Shanghai (2007)
4. Cichocki, A., Washizawa, Y., Rutkowski, T., Bakardjian, H., Phan, A.H., Choi, S., Lee, H., Zhao, Q., Zhang, L., Li, Y.: Noninvasive BCIs: Multiway signal-processing array decompositions. Computer 41(10), 34–42 (2008)
5. Guger, C., Daban, S., Sellers, E., Holzner, C., Krausz, G., Carabalona, R., Gramatica, F., Edlinger, G.: How many people are able to control a P300-based brain-computer interface (BCI)? Neuroscience Letters 462(1), 94–98 (2009)
6. Hjorth, B.: EEG analysis based on time domain properties. Electroencephalography and Clinical Neurophysiology 29, 306–310 (1970)
7. Huang, N., Shen, Z., Long, S., Wu, M., Shih, H., Zheng, Q., Yen, N.C., Tung, C., Liu, H.: The empirical mode decomposition and the Hilbert spectrum for nonlinear and non-stationary time series analysis. Proceedings of the Royal Society A: Mathematical, Physical and Engineering Sciences 454(1971), 903–995 (1988)
8. Niedermeyer, E., Da Silva, F.L. (eds.): Electroencephalography: Basic Principles, Clinical Applications, and Related Fields, 5th edn. Lippincott Williams & Wilkins, Baltimore (2004)

9. Plourde, G.: Auditory evoked potentials. Best Practice & Research Clinical Anaesthesiology 20(1), 129–139 (2006)
10. R Development Core Team: R: A Language and Environment for Statistical Computing. R Foundation for Statistical Computing, Vienna, Austria (2008), http://www.R-project.org, http://www.R-project.org
11. Ross, B., Picton, T.W., Herdman, A.T., Hillyard, S.A., Pantev, C.: The effect of attention on the auditory steady-state response. Neurology and Clinical Neurophysiology 22, 1–4 (2004)
12. Rutkowski, T.M., Cichocki, A., Mandic, D.P.: Information Fusion for Perceptual Feedback: A Brain Activity Sonification Approach. In: Signal Processing Techniques for Knowledge Extraction and Information Fusion. Signals and Communication, pp. 261–274. Springer, Heidelberg (April 2008)
13. Rutkowski, T.M., Cichocki, A., Mandic, D.P.: Spatial auditory paradigms for brain computer/machine interfacing. In: Proceedings of International Workshop on the Principles And Applications of Spatial Hearing 2009 (IWPASH 2009), Miyagi-Zao Royal Hotel, Sendai, Japan, p. 5 (November 11-13, 2009), http://dx.doi.org/10.1142/9789814299312_0025
14. Rutkowski, T.M., Cichocki, A., Tanaka, T., Mandic, D.P., Cao, J., Ralescu, A.L.: Multichannel spectral pattern separation - an EEG processing application. In: Proceedings of the 2009 IEEE International Conference on Acoustics, Speech, and Signal Processing (ICASSP 2009), pp. 373–376. IEEE Press, Taipei (2009)
15. Rutkowski, T.M., Tanaka, T., Zhao, Q., Cichocki, A.: Spatial auditory BCI/BMI paradigm - Multichannel EMD approach to brain responses estimation. In: Proceedings of the Second APSIPA Annual Summit and Conference (APSIPA ASC 2010), December 14-17, pp. 197–202. APSIPA, Biopolis (2010)
16. Schlögl, A., Brunner, C.: Biosig: A free and open source software library for BCI research. Computer 41(10), 44–50 (2008)
17. Schreuder, M., Blankertz, B., Tangermann, M.: A new auditory multi-class brain-computer interface paradigm: Spatial hearing as an informative cue. PLoS ONE 5(4), e9813 (2010), http://dx.doi.org/10.1371%2Fjournal.pone.0009813
18. Stach, B.A.: The auditory steady-state response: A primer. The Hearing Journal 55(9), 10–18 (2002)
19. Wellcome Trust Centre for Neuroimaging: Statistical parametric mapping - SPM8 package (2010), http://www.fil.ion.ucl.ac.uk/spm/, http://www.fil.ion.ucl.ac.uk/spm/
20. Zhao, Q., Rutkowski, T., Zhang, L., Cichocki, A.: Generalized optimal spatial filtering using a kernel approach with application to EEG classification. Cognitive Neurodynamics 4(4), 355–358 (2010), http://dx.doi.org/10.1007/s11571-010-9125-x

Noncontact Haptic Interface Using Ultrasound

Hiroyuki Shinoda

The University of Tokyo
7-3-1 Hongo, Bunkyo-ku, Tokyo 113-8656 Japan
shino@alab.t.u-tokyo.ac.jp

Abstract. The current haptic technologies in 1-to-1 teleoperations, mobile communications, and computer games have already moved into a phase of practical use. One of the next attractive challenges is haptic assistance to unspecified people in public spaces. The potential demands for haptic assistance include alarming and guiding people, delivering knowledge and experiences, collecting people's intentions, and offering entertainment in public spaces. We need a technological leap from the conventional mechanical methods to enable ordinary people to enjoy public haptic assistance without special devices held in their hands. In this keynote speech, a non-contact tactile display using airborne ultrasound is introduced as a solution. Radiant pressure by convergent ultrasound beams produces tactile sensations on bare skin. It is even possible to apply haptic stimulations to people moving around in an open space. Combining the tactile display with 3D images realizes programmable 3D interfaces with tactile responses. The basic principle, characteristics, and limitations are explained. Also, the future of noncontact haptics, including remote haptic sensing and haptic sharing, will be discussed.

Keywords: Haptic interface, remote haptic display, ultrasound tactile display, haptic sharing.

1   Introduction

The current tactile feedback hardware is classified into three categories. The first one is adding computed reaction forces to the devices that originally exist for operation, such as steering wheels and operating levers. The main purpose is to make the operation easier and sometimes it is used for enhancing the reality of simulator training. The second category is general-purpose force displays using multi-degree-of-freedom link mechanisms mounted on the floors or tables as PHANTOM® Haptic Device. A user holds the arm top and moves it freely to feel the contact with virtual objects by the reaction forces controlled by a computer. The third category is wearable force and cutaneous displays. In this category, various tactile feedbacks are realized by simple device structures using the properties of the human tactile perception including illusions [1]. The deformations of the handheld or glove-like devices display forces by touch [2][3]. Touch-panels and buttons vibrate depending on the finger positions for displaying tactile response [4]. Electrical stimulations give tactile feedbacks [5][6] with no mechanical movements. These devices are wearable

E.W. Cooper et al. (Eds.): HAID 2011, LNCS 6851, pp. 120–127, 2011.

in principle, and sometimes is also used being fixed on the surfaces of the environments [7].

As a common feature of currently available tactile display systems, they need direct contact of the human skins to some display devices. The nature has limited their applications to special ones in which people touch intentionally the display devices embedded in the environment or they wear special portable devices in advance. This paper introduces a method to stimulate our bare hands using airborne ultrasound. The system generates small forces remotely to unconstrained hands. In principle, a wide-aperture ultrasound phased array enables haptic stimulations to people moving around in an open space. In this paper, the principle and properties of the non-contact tactile display are introduced. The potential applications and new problems posed by remote haptics are discussed.

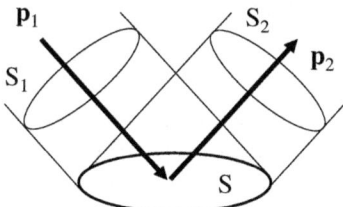

Fig. 1. Radiation pressure

2 Noncontact Tactile Display

Before the work of [8] by Iwamoto et al. of our laboratory, the only non-contact tactile display is that of air jet. The theoretical limitation of air-jet method resides in the trade-off between the work space volume and the spatial resolution of tactile stimulation. For example, it is easy to make a jet with a radius of 50 cm reach 1m, while it is virtually impossible to make a jet with 5mm radius do the same. As a result, we have to put our hand close to the jet nozzles if we want to display detailed force distributions.

Another method using the air as the force transmission medium is use of airborne ultrasound. A force spot is produced on the skin with radiation pressure produced by a converging beam generated from a phased array. Although the acceptable maximal pressure is 0.6N/cm^2 for the safety, a work space larger than 1m is possible using a large aperture phased array. It has a temporal bandwidth of pressure change more than 1kHz, and fast spatial movement of the force distribution is possible.

2.1 Ultrasound Radiation Pressure

In linear acoustics, the average of pressure is equal to 0. Significant radiation pressure [9] proportional to the sound power is observed for a large amplitude sound. Quantitatively, the radiation pressure is given as

$$\mathbf{f} = \frac{1}{c}(S_1\mathbf{p}_1 - S_2\mathbf{p}_2) \qquad [N] \qquad (1)$$

where $\mathbf{f}$ [N] is the force applied to area S as shown in Fig. 1, $\mathbf{p}_1$ [W/m^2] the incident power stream through the area S_1 onto S, $\mathbf{p}_2$ [W/m^2] the power stream reflected by S, and c the sound velocity. Since the applied force is proportional to the acoustic energy density on the surface, we can control the force and its spatial distribution on the skin by the intensity and the wave front geometry of the acoustic wave. We expect the applied force can produce a wide variety of tactile feeling since the ultrasound frequency, 40kHz in our prototype, is much larger than the bandwidth of the human tactile sensation. The delay of stimulation from the sound propagation $\tau = D/c$, where D is the propagation distance, is 3ms for $D = 1$m. The delay is not always negligible in dynamic feedback but it is acceptable in many applications. The limitations of this method are summarized as follows.

2.2 Maximal Force

As shown in Eq. (1), the total force by the radiation pressure is proportional to the total power of the incident acoustic wave. For example, 1gf = 0.01N requires 0.5×0.01N×340m/s = 1.7W in the case of vertical incidence to the surface and complete reflection. Considering the efficiency of the ultrasound transducers, the power consumption is comparable to that of indoor lighting. Temporal average of the consumed power is much smaller since the force is produced only at the moment of touch. However, it can be a problem in installation to mobile devices.

The safety for the human body is the most important factor to be considered. The safety standard of the ultrasound is still under discussions. In a wide range of safety standards, the conservative standard is around 100mW/cm^2 in the literatures [10]. Most of the incident ultrasound is reflected on the skin surface and 0.1% of incident sound is absorbed in the body. Therefore the incident airborne ultrasound power corresponding to 100mW/cm^2 transmission into the skin is $p = 100$W/cm^2 whose radiation pressure is $2p/c = 0.6$N/cm^2 (= 60gf/cm^2). This is the theoretical limit of displayable pressure by this method.

The damage to ears should be ensured by the other standard [11]. In a practical system, it is desirable that our ears are not exposed to strong ultrasounds.

2.3 Work Space and Spatial Resolution

The factors to decide the work space and spatial resolution are ultrasound wavelength λ, ultrasound attenuation length L, and diameter W of the phased array aperture. The minimal diameter of the displayed force spot is comparable to the wavelength λ. The highest resolution is attained when the distance between the phased array and the display point is comparable to W or less. Fig. 2 shows the measurement results of radiation pressure by Hoshi et al. [12]. 18×18 = 324 ultrasound transducers are arranged in 18cm×18cm square area. The radiation pressure is measured in a plane 20cm distant from the phased array. The spot diameter looks comparable to the wavelength 8mm for 40kHz ultrasound. If we increase the distance D from the phased array, the spot radius increases inverse-proportional to

$$\sin \theta = \frac{W/2}{\sqrt{D^2 + (W/2)^2}} \tag{2}$$

There is also a trade-off between the resolution and the work space in the ultrasound tactile display. In order to increase the resolution, we should use a higher frequency of ultrasound. On the other hand, heightening the frequency causes attenuation of the ultrasound, which shortens the displayable distance from the phased array. The reason why we use 40kHz ultrasound in our prototype is the attenuation length is relatively large (1dB/m). If we make the frequency n times higher, attenuation length L becomes smaller by $1/n^2$. Therefore if a half meter of work space is necessary, we cannot use a much higher frequency than 40kHz. The 1cm resolution is a rough practical standard of this method.

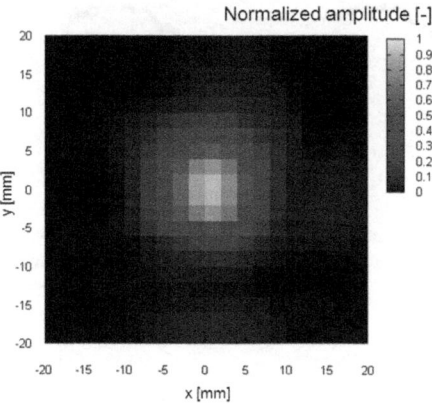

(a) Normalized radiation pressure measured on a plane 20 cm apart from the phased array.

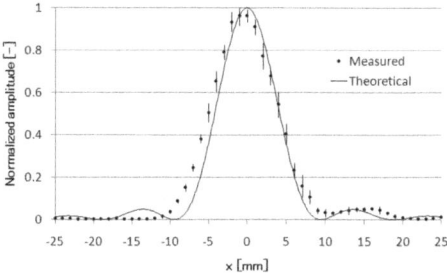

(b) Normalized radiation pressure measured at y = 0.

Fig. 2. Results of radiation pressure measurement by Hoshi et al. [12].

Fig. 3 shows the temporal waveforms of the acoustic pressure and the radiation pressure. The Input voltage to the transducers is a series of 40kHz rectangular waves that have a constant amplitude during 0 – 5ms and 10 – 15ms. The acoustic and radiation pressure is measured at the center of the focal point. Fig. 3(b) shows that the radiation pressure rises within 1ms. Since the used ultrasound transducer is a resonant type, the acoustic amplitude rises with the time constant of 0.3ms as shown in Fig. 3(b) - CH1. The radiation pressure of CH2 looks proportional to the square of the sound pressure. The time constant shorter than 1ms is satisfactory for tactile display.

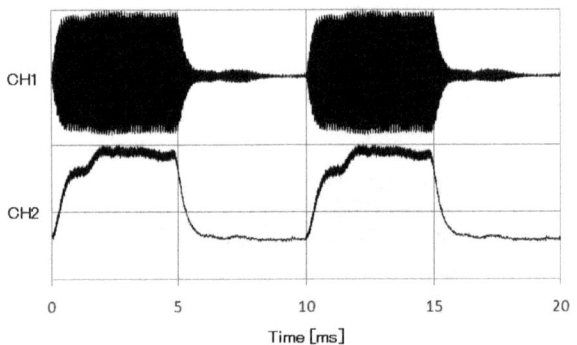

(a)   Modulated waveforms measured at focal point. Ultrasound (CH1) and radiation pressure (CH2).

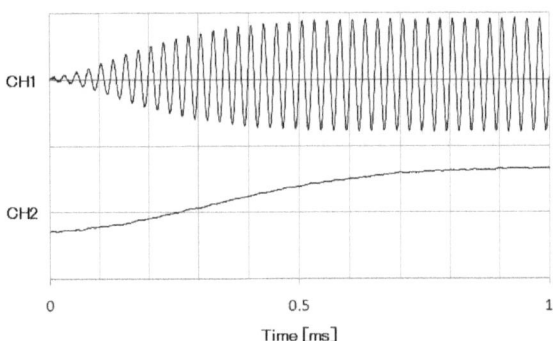

(b)   Closeup of (a) from 0 to 1 ms.

Fig. 3. Temporal waveform of radiation pressure [12]

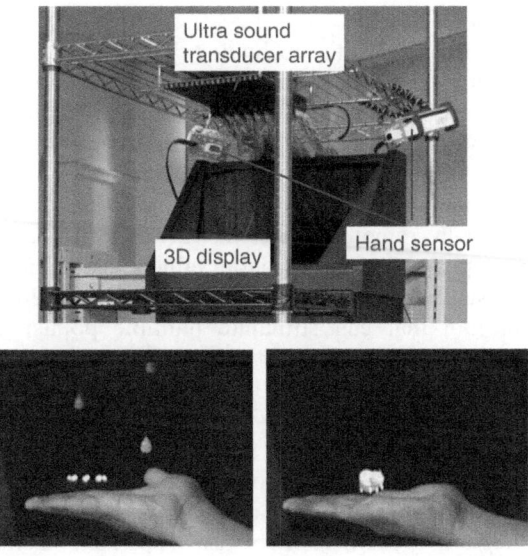

Fig. 4. Examples of 3D images with tactile responses. The upper photo shows the system overview [12].

3   Future Haptic Interaction Using Noncontact Tactile Display

Released from the conventional physical constraint, the direct contact to the device, we can envision new application fields of haptics. The potential applications are summarized as follows.

Active Touch Assistance
Active touch sensation is evoked when we actively touch objects to manipulate or to intentionally sense it. An application field of ultrasound tactile display is to add tactile response to active touch action for floating visual images, which makes visual floating images touchable. The prototype system is shown in Fig. 4. Straightforward applications of such touchable images will be seen in hospitals, for example. Floating button images in reception lounges will be useful as non-contact touch panels for preventing contiguous infection among patients. In operation rooms, doctors can access the computer system with dirty hands.

Touchable floating images can enhance the dimension of a computer interface device from two-dimensional as touch panel to three-dimensional. We can freely locate virtual interface devices around us, and interact with them anywhere in the workspace and anytime necessary, in principle.

The objects people interact with are not always floating images. The radiation pressure can induce vibrations to light-weight real objects around us. For example, we can make a simple paper be an interface device in ambient environments that senses the hand positions and projects images on the paper, as well as producing tactile responses. The sound accompanied with the contact can be easily superimposed by the ultrasound.

Passive Touch Assistance

Passive touch assistance by haptic technology is an unexplored and promising application field. Haptics is potentially the quickest and most certain modality to inform the individuals of the appropriate ways of actions. Audio alarming is effective in many cases. But the signal reaches unconcerned persons and it takes time and requires intellectual process to understand how to react to the circumstances. Haptic signal can provide instantaneous instruction for individual persons. Remote haptic display can realize such remote tactile instructions for car drivers, people in emergency, machine operators, etc.. Teaching athletic skills and knacks of dynamic motions by haptic assistance is also an attractive challenge. Remote haptic display will be a powerful tool that can stimulate multiple points of the skin without constraining human's actions.

Haptic-Sharing Assistance

Remote haptic communication is also an attractive application. As audio and visual channels, remote haptics enables us to communicate with remote people by haptic sense. If people are within a coverage area of a large aperture ultrasound display, we can send tactile signal to remote persons. The next theme following 1-to1 communication will be haptic sharing. Remote haptics enables multiple people who happen to be there to share tactile information.

The new theme, haptic sharing poses another problem of remote haptics, that is, remote haptic sensing. In order to share haptic information of real and unknown objects among multiple people, we need remote sensors that model the haptic properties of the objects in real time. In this talk, our recent research of remote haptic sensing [13] is also introduced. The identical ultrasound phased array is used for sensing the surface elasticity. The future of haptic-sharing realized by remote haptics is discussed.

References

1. Hayward, V.: A Brief Taxonomy of Tactile Illusions and Demonstrations That Can Be Done In a Hardware Store. Brain Research Bulletin 75, 742–752 (2008)
2. Kamuro, S., Minamizawa, K., Kawakami, N., Tachi, S.: Pen de touch. In: ACM SIGGRAPH 2009 Emerging Technologies (2009)
3. Sato, K., Minamizawa, K., Kawakami, N., Tachi, S.: Haptic Telexistence. In: Proc. 34th Int. Conf. on Computer Graphics and Interactive Techniques (ACM SIGGRAPH 2007), Emerging Technologies, article no. 10 (2007)
4. Immersion Corporation website
5. Kajimoto, H., Kawakami, N., Maeda, T., Tachi, S.: Tactile Feeling Display Using Functional Electrical Stimulation. In: Proc. the 9th Int. Conf. on Artificial Reality and Telexistence, pp. 107–114 (1999)
6. E-Sense^{TM}, Senseg website
7. Goldish, L.H., Taylor, H.E.: The Optacon: A Valuable Device for Blind Persons. New Outlook for the Blind 68(2), 49–56 (1974)
8. Iwamoto, T., Tatezono, M., Shinoda, H.: Non-contact Method for Producing Tactile Sensation Using Airborne Ultrasound. In: Ferre, M. (ed.) EuroHaptics 2008. LNCS, vol. 5024, pp. 504–513. Springer, Heidelberg (2008)

9. Awatani, J.: Studies on Acoustic Radiation Pressure. I (General Considerations). J. Acoust. Soc. Am. 27(2), 278–281 (1955)
10. Creasy, R.K., Resnik, R., Iams, J.D.: Maternal-Fetal Medicine, Saunders (1999)
11. Howard, C.Q., Hansen, C.H., Zander, A.C.: A Review of Current Ultrasound Exposure Limits. The Journal of Occupational Health and Safety of Australia and New Zealand 21(3), 253–257 (2005)
12. Hoshi, T., Takahashi, M., Iwamoto, T., Shinoda, H.: Non–contact Tactile Display Based on Radiation Pressure of Airborne Ultrasound. IEEE Transactions on Haptics 3(3), 155–165 (2010)
13. Fujiwara, M., Nakatsuma, K., Takahashi, M., Shinoda, H.: Remote Measurement of Surface Compliance Distribution Using Ultrasound Radiation Pressure. In: World Haptics Conference 2011, Istanbul, Turkey (to be published in June 2011)

Smell-Based Memory Recollection and Communication Support

Yusuke Kita and Yoshio Nakatani

Graduate School of Science and Engineering, Ritsumeikan University
cc006061@ed.ritsumei.ac.jp, nakatani@is.ritsumei.ac.jp

Abstract. Many victims of The Great Best Japan Earthquake lost many precious mementos. Such losses can result in more time being required to recover emotionally and mentally. This paper proposes an effective reminder management system using smell. The system focuses support for recollecting fond memories. Preliminary experiments using a device that produces smell showed that it was effective to help recall fond memories by smell. This system encourages us to remember fond memories by inducing specific smells, recording smells in a system, and allowing communication between people who have similar experiences.

Keywords: fond memories, recollection, communication, olfactory modality.

1 Introduction

Memories and mementos are accumulated every day. Digital cameras and cell phones equipped with camera functions are now widely used, allowing people to easily record their individual experiences in everyday life and an unprecedented number of photographs being stored. In response to this trend, Nojima[1] has emphasized the importance of memento administration and proposed a type of memory engineering for use in organizing and administering rapidly increasing mementos. Memory engineering aims to create an engineering support framework for the efficient and effective administration, storage, and utilization of vast numbers of mementos, especially pictures and videos.

The Great East Japan Earthquake resulted in the victims of the disasters having lost precious mementos through the tsunami, fire, and collapse of their houses. The mementos referred to here can include those involving precious family members, the houses in which they were born and raised, places they used to play as children, familiar surroundings such as neighbors and friends, as well as the diaries, pictures, albums, and videos used to record all of them. The common belief is that for victims of disasters losing those mementos can result in more time being required for them to recover mentally because they feel a sense of loss of the time they spent in their lives, which they had stored in the form of mementos, resulting from having lost the mementos. In many cases, they may therefore be afraid that they will no longer be able to recollect the memories on which their identity is based [2]. People do not only look to the future but also live in the present based on trust in themselves which is consistent throughout their life, from birth right through to the present. One reason

E.W. Cooper et al. (Eds.): HAID 2011, LNCS 6851, pp. 128–134, 2011.
© Springer-Verlag Berlin Heidelberg 2011

elderly victims of disasters may take longer to recover mentally than younger people can be easily understood to be that the former have had longer lives, with the resulting loss for the former therefore being bigger than with the latter. In many cases people losing continuity in their lives due to disasters or accidents can give rise to fear and make them incapable of starting a new life. Starting a new life requires a solid foundation of their identity, in which going back over (recalling) past enjoyable episodes in their lives is both necessary and important [3]. In the case of the Great East Japan Earthquake, the importance of the mementos has been publicly recognized and many "memory search squads" were organized from volunteer groups [4]. The groups are involved in the volunteer activities of searching for photo albums and commemorative objects from the debris in areas with heavy tsunami damage. In the afflicted areas, activities have been organized with the specific goal of recovering photographs that evoke memories and returning them to their owners. Many of the disaster victims state that, "I feel I can push myself just a little harder if I can receive the picture I cherish, even if it is just one picture", thus implying that the mementos are of significant meaning to the victims of the disasters.

The present study involves the establishment of concepts for systems used to induce memory recollection and thus support the victims of disasters who have lost mementos by supporting that recollection using an alternative memory recollection trigger. The target situation of this study is the opposite of conventional memory engineering and therefore requires a rather different approach. The concept of the system involves pictures of common sightseeing spots, maps, old popular music, the smell of food and other things, and other types of stimulation being used to promote the recollection of memories. The system also utilizes humming as an unconscious activity in everyday life to promote the recollection of any music related memories. The system then records the content of the recollections, thus supporting communication with others with similar experiences. This paper proposes a system that focuses on supporting memories being recollected with elicitation that employs the sense of smell.

2 Related Studies

Nakatani [3] proposed a framework for use in supporting the reconstruction of the memories of the victims of disasters. The framework provided triggers for use in recalling memories, including information on the time, place, event, names of individuals, etc., and feelings [4]. The triggers used in that recollection play a significant role in recalling memories, with a strong link being necessary between the triggers and the memories.

Memory engineering often utilizes pictures as a major trigger in recalling memories [5]. Pictures can visually evoke an image and thus are quite effective in memory recollection and communication support. However, the method would be ineffective in this study as it is highly likely that the victims of the disasters covered have typically lost all their pictures. In addition, if the victims of disasters have not recovered from the shock, recalled memories from pictures can result in adverse effects.

Music was also studied as a trigger in place of pictures [6]. Music, for example popular music, can often be common to everybody and hence easily shared with others. Music is also often closely related to memories and people can often easily recall a memory merely by listening to and humming tunes. The system proposed in [6] identifies a hummed tune and provides the name of the hummed song and its singer, together with the related data, such as his or her own related memories and those of other users linked to the tune in the memory database, similar tunes of the same classification, and tunes of the same period. Based on these data, the system promotes memory recollection of the period and recommends other tunes which are favored by other users who love the hummed tune, as new memory triggers. However, the content of memory related to music can significantly vary, in some cases depending on the individual, thereby making the sharing of memories somewhat difficult.

In addition to the triggers mentioned above smell was also studied as a trigger of memories. Smell can be easily connected to a specific memory and it is said that the sense of smell is the most effective with long-term memories, in particular. In this study images and text were used as triggers in addition to smells in supporting the communication of memories. However, the objects that users recalled from a smell were not very consistent with the images and text presented by the system in relation to that smell, and hence, the system did not prove to be very effective.

3   Overview of the System

This study concerns the establishment of support for memories being recollected and communicated with a focus on the close relationship between a smell and long-term memory. People often recognize a smell, particularly when food related, and recall an experience as a memory after smelling the same smell. This study therefore focused on food related smells. We believe that a system for making smells that are familiar to users can effectively promote the recollection of memories.

This study utilized the Aromageur, developed by Mirapro Corporation [7], to produce the smells (Figure 1). The equipment can control the smell, including its strength or weakness, by blending up to six types of essential oils and flavors in specific proportions. The equipment can also easily be used to blend original smells. Furthermore, the blend used can then be saved as electronic data, and hence can be invoked and reproduced at a later time.

3.1   Recommending a Smell That Suits the Preference of Users

The expectation was that releasing a smell that suits the user from the system would effectively promote the recollection of memories and support communication. Morphological analysis was used to analyze the preference of users. The morphological analysis used in the system extracts nouns from the text and identifies any words concerning food from among them. The system then extracts any words that are particularly popular as well as those that can be closely linked to the memories of users.

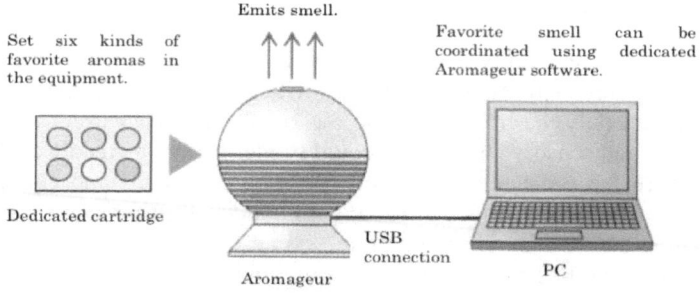

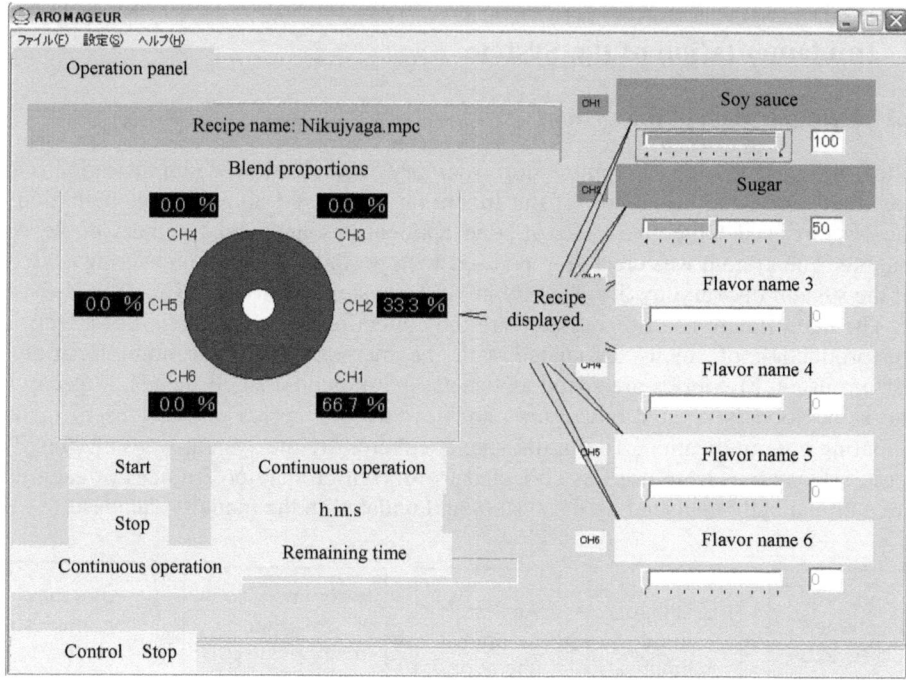

Fig. 1. Experimental setup and its user interface

The flow of use will now be explained. The system utilizes Twitter [8] through which it collects the tweets (public posts of 140 characters or less) of users, automatically extracts keywords for use in the morphological analysis, and the produce smells related to the keywords thus extracted. In this step an image related to the keyword is also shown. If the user does recollect a memory the system then asks the user to tweet the recipe of the smell and details on the memory evoked. The system then saves the details of the memory and related smell. The tweets can additionally draw the interest of other users, thus initiating conversations, which thereby supports communication.

3.2 Sharing Memories via Use of Smell and Images

The system assumes usage mainly during mealtimes and at people's homes. For example, people often take pictures and tweet via Twitter when eating sweets or fruit. If they could tweet not only the image but also the smell, then other users would be able to receive visual and sensory stimuli that could trigger memories recollected. The situation exists where the same image of food has different smells and conversely almost the same smell different images of food, with that small difference then being capable of promoting active conversation among several users. We therefore believe that grouping tweets according to the smell of food could be used to promote active communication among users.

4 Implementation of the System

4.1 Configuration of the System

The system provides support for memory recollection, administration, and communication via utilization of the functions mentioned above. Implementation of the system used Objective-C for iPhone applications and php for the Google App Engine. The system was created to be used with portable devices in ensuring easy use of the system in everyday life. An outline of the system is shown in Fig. 2.

The main functions of this system are the collection and organization of memories, the production of smells associated with the memories, and the administration of system users. Memories are saved as tweets, pictures, and smell blends. A group for the same food is created and users can view the memories of other users in thus initiating communication. The initial smells covered by the system were of fruit. The basic information from users is collected from Twitter. The preferences of each user are automatically analyzed by the system and updated in the memory database.

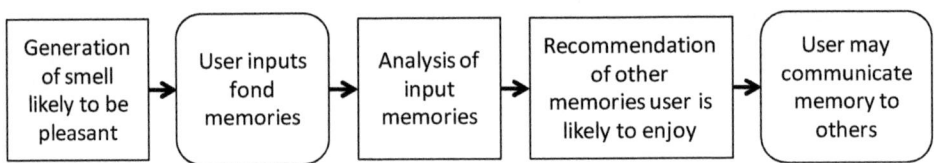

Fig. 2. The Processing flow of the proposed system

The following is a description of a typical use case example for the system. The user first logs on to the system via their Twitter account. The system then obtains past tweets of the user and analyzes them. The results of the analysis of the user's previous posts is then used to produce a smell. If the user recalls something they may then tweet the details to the system, with the smell needing to be tweeted as well. The user can browse both their own and other users' tweets via the system.

In addition, the user includes a picture and smell with a tweet when they eat something. Other users can then view the tweet, use it to recall something, and then tweet the details with a picture and smell. This then initiates communication within a group of users that have tweeted on similar food. We believe that other users will then join the tweet concerning the pictures and smell, thus making the conversation more active.

4.2 Preliminary Experiments

Two trial studies were conducted to test the system and develop suitable protocols for future experiments. The first experiment took place in which a blend of the smell of that children's favorite, curry and rice, was produced using Aromageur to verify whether it would result in any memory being recollected. All four male university students who participated in this experiment reported recognizing the foods expressed by the device and that the smell of food was properly blended. The experience of each smell also resulted in the recollection of specific memories related to that smell. An unexpected result was that many of the experimental subjects reported that the smell produced from the Aromageur was "stronger" than that of the actual food itself. One possible explanation for this perceived discrepancy may have been that the smells produced by the device have no visual focus. This result may be the first known observation of an olfactory illusion that smells are experienced as stronger when the object to which the smell is attributed is not visible, even though the origin of the smell is with the visual field of the observer. The smell remained within the space for about 30 minutes, thereby making it difficult to blend several kinds of smells in the same experiment. Further efforts will need to take place in implementing more experiments on the recollection of memories via the use of smell.

Another preliminary experiment took place with communication concerning food. Fifteen university students were involved in the experiment. This slightly larger study found that the topic of food, in addition to the smells, was sufficient to trigger fond memories. This study confirmed that the topic of food was very good trigger to recall fond memories and that communication concerning food encourages recollecting fond memories. However, this study also found that subjects were often more likely to recall food from fond memories than fond memories from food.

5 Conclusions

Experiments took place on supporting the recollection of memories via use of the abovementioned system. Preliminary experiments found important relationships between smell and fond memories. A smaller preliminary study found that subjects report stronger smells when an object to which the smell may be attributed is not visually apparent, a possible olfactory illusion not yet known to have been reported. This study also experienced some of the difficulties of smell display research, most notably the temporal resolution issue and how to deal with lingering smells, one which, unlike the olfactory illusion reported, is likely to have some solutions in real life smell experiments but which needs to be revamped for use with smell displays. A second, larger study found that the strong roots of food in human communication, and the relationship of food to the sense of smell, make the use of smell for the recollection of memories problematic. The study found that smells thought to be related to food were just as likely or more likely to generate memories of the food itself. So targeting specific memories, for example a pleasant event from the past, has to solve the problem of distracting memories of the object to which the smell was attributed at the time. We intend to continue to verify whether smells can effectively promote recollection and communication of memories.

References

1. Nojima, H., Harada, E.: Cognitive Science for Inside the House. In: Memory Engineering, Shin-yo-sha, ch. 12, pp. 269–288 (2004)
2. Hirose, H.: Why Do People Fail to Escape? – Disaster Psychology, Shin-Eisha (2004)
3. Nakatani, Y.: Support System for Reconstructing Fond Memories Lost in Disasters. In: Proceedings of HCI International, pp. 1–10 (2005)
4. Memories Search Squad Recruits Members to Search the Rubble of Minamisanriku, Sankei News, Life Section (March 27, 2011) (in Japanese)
5. Yamashita, K., Nojima, H.: Portable Personal Memory for Communication (2). In: Human Interface Symposium 2002, pp. 503–506 (2002) (in Japanese)
6. Kita, Y., Nakatani, Y.: Recall and Communication Support System of Reminiscence Triggered by Humming. In: Proceedings of the 14th International Conference on Human-Computer Interaction (HCI International 2011), Hilton Orlando Bonnet Creek, Orlando, Florida, USA, pp. 323–330 (2011)
7. MIRAPRO Corporation: Aromageur,
   http://www.mirapro.co.jp/gyomu/aroma.html (in Japanese)
8. Twitter, https://twitter.com/

Author Index